I SURVIVED
12+ YEARS AFTER
A STROKE
AND YOU CAN TOO

STROKE RECOVERY THROUGH REHABILITATION

GOPI A. TEJWANI, PH. D.

authorHOUSE®

AuthorHouse™
1663 Liberty Drive
Bloomington, IN 47403
www.authorhouse.com
Phone: 833-262-8899

Published by AuthorHouse 09/29/2020

ISBN: 978-1-6655-0215-3 (sc)
ISBN: 978-1-6655-0216-0 (hc)
ISBN: 978-1-6655-0285-6 (e)

Library of Congress Control Number: 2020919076

Print information available on the last page.

CONTENTS

PREFACE

October 7, 2008, was a day like any other till the moment a devastating stroke in my brain stem changed my life forever.

With the stroke, began a new phase in my life—one that started with a six-week-long stay in the hospital, of which two weeks were in a coma. When I regained my senses after two weeks I was perplexed as to what and how it happened. I started asking myself why me? Is this the end of my life? All of a sudden, my limbs were not working, I could not eat on my own, I could barely stand, and my speech was slurred so much so that most people had a hard time understanding me. My stroke left me in a wheelchair for three months, six months on sick leave from work, and without the ability to drive for two whole years.

This book is about my twelve-year struggle with stroke recovery beginning from the time I first opened my eyes at Dodd Hall rehabilitation hospital. Prior to this, I only remember the first five seconds following the stroke and have vague recollections of the first thirty minutes when the paramedics came. My dreams when I was in a coma remain vivid technicolor! I am still at loss to explain all the dreams, though few of them correlate with my medical disorders at the time, such as the urinary infection. The book describes the assistance I received from various therapists, family, and friends.

In this book, I will describe in detail the numerous problems I suffered as a result of the stroke, such as paralysis of the right side of my body, balance issues, insomnia, double vision, an elevated heart rate, among a host of other problems. Today, I am dependent on a right Ankle-Foot-Orthotics (AFO) and a walking cane. I will also discuss the various mental and emotional issues that I faced after the stroke.

This book is my journey of recovery and self-healing through hard work, medical assistance, and prayer over twelve years. I want to share my experiences in the hope that it can help another person in a similar predicament. The book talks about gamma knife surgery, massage therapy, and Botox injections, as well as the value of these procedures in the treatment of a stroke.

Why did I write this book?

The reasons for writing this book are manifold. For all stroke victims out there who are asking "why me?" I just want to say that you are not alone. If there is one thing I want to achieve through this book is to convey the message that even though a stroke can be debilitating but it is not the end of life.

Do not ask yourself: Did I deserve a stroke? It is a fruitless question. One has to toughen up. Be optimistic. And do your best. Remember that there are people who are worse off than you, so be grateful for what you have. When I had my stroke, I thought that it was the end of my life. I could barely stand up straight and needed the help of three people to help me walk twenty feet! I was being fed through a feeding tube from my abdomen into the stomach. But I didn't give up. With support from my wonderful family and friends, I worked very hard; took therapy; and stayed optimistic.

If I can inspire even one person to not to give up hope and double their efforts, I have achieved my goal. I hope that this book serves a valuable tool to millions of stroke patients, their families, and friends, and brings back the joy in their life.

1

JUST ANOTHER DAY

It was an ordinary Tuesday afternoon.

I had just stepped into my office at the Ohio State University (also called the OSU), where I had been teaching for more than three decades. The day seemed full of promise. I was feeling particularly upbeat and had even put on a new shirt and tie. No reason, really. Or, perhaps it was because I was subconsciously excited about my upcoming vacation to South Africa with my wife, Sarla, and friends. Our bookings were all done. The tour agency we had sought help from was well known in their field. Yes, I was excited. All that was left to do was pack our bags. Life was good. I thought to myself, it was going to be a good day.

A couple of hours later, I still had a spring in my steps. I was sixty-two years old and happy. The OSU was a second home to me. I knew everyone around, and they knew me. Every time I stepped out of my office, there was usually someone who would wave a hello. "Hello Dr. Tejwani, how are you?" I would always smile back in acknowledgment. Today was no different. I bumped into a few familiar faces on the way. This is how it was always.

At sharp 1 pm, I opened my lunch box to eat. It was my favorite meal of rice and shrimps. I had just started to eat when suddenly, I remembered the date. *October 7, 2008!* It was my friend Dr. Ashok Singh's birthday. Ashok and I go back a long way. He was a fellow graduate student at the All India Institute of Medical Sciences in New Delhi in the early 1970s. I always remember his birthday. Without wasting a minute more, I promptly took out my phone and dialed his number. The phone buzzed for a few seconds before I heard the familiar voice at the other end. "Hello! Hello!"

"Ashok! Happy birthday!"

Ashok was happy to hear from me as he always was. We had a short conversation and then I hung up. While speaking with Ashok, it occurred to me that I had not paid three police penalty tickets when I had visited him in Chicago a few months back. This was because I was on the main highway and the toll booths were on the side of the road. I had simply zoomed past without paying my dues. I decided to clear them immediately.

I opened the browser of my Personal Computer to search for the penalty-paying site. Ah! There it was. Just when I took out my credit card to pay, my office phone rang out. It was a student from my Pharmacology 600 course. He needed some clarification on a topic I had been teaching recently. We were speaking for a few minutes when I thought I heard him scream. But why?

"Dr. Tejwani! You are not making any sense! Dr. Tejwani!"

Time seemed to move in slow motion, and I thought to myself. *But why? Why doesn't he understand? Why am I not making any sense?* And then, all of a sudden, as if a cloud had been lifted from my senses, I heard myself out loud.

"Yaaaaaaaaaaa…"

Then, the phone fell from my hands and I passed out on the floor.

2

WHAT IS A STROKE?

Every year in the United States, an average of 800,000 people are victims of stroke, of which about 130,000 die. Undoubtedly, this is a large number.

But let us first understand what a stroke is.

The brain is a highly vascular organ, which requires a constant supply of oxygen to nourish it. Oxygenated blood is carried through arteries originating in the heart. The brain also contains the pituitary gland, which plays a major role in regulating vital functions and the general well-being of the body. For this reason, it is sometimes called the master gland of the human body. Lack of oxygenated blood to the brain causes severe damage to the organ and is deemed a medical emergency. When the supply of oxygen to the brain is cut off, a sudden loss of brain function occurs. This condition is called a stroke.

There are two primary factors that lead to a stroke—first, inadequate supply of oxygenated blood to the brain due to a blood clot and second, rupture of blood vessels in the brain. The first causes an ischemic stroke and the second, a hemorrhagic stroke. There is also a third type called Transient Ischemic Attack (TIA), which is a mini-stroke because the effects of this stroke disappear within twenty-four hours.

About eighty-seven percent of all stroke victims are said to suffer from ischemic stroke, which occurs due to an inadequate supply of oxygenated blood to the brain. In this type of stroke, ischemia—or lack of delivery of oxygenated blood to the brain—ensues because of a clot in a blood vessel in the brain. There are two ways this can happen. In the first instance, the clot may occur due to a thrombus, which is a blood clot that forms on the wall of a blood vessel supplying oxygenated blood to the brain. Or, it could be the result of an embolism, in which a dislodged clot from another part of the body reaches the brain. When a clot travels through a blood vessel to the brain and occludes its blood supply, it is called an embolus. Either way, it causes damage to the brain tissue, and the brain's function of maintaining equilibrium in the body is hampered. It is believed that about thirty to forty thousand brain cells die per second due to ischemia if the patient does not get immediate help.

The second and more severe type of stroke is a hemorrhagic stroke. In this type of stroke, a blood vessel supplying oxygenated blood supply to the brain is ruptured, resulting in loss of oxygen to the brain as well as the development of pressure in the brain tissue causing premature death of brain cells. Only thirteen percent of stroke victims suffer from this type of stroke—I happened to be a part of this small percentage.

The third type is a transient ischemic attack (TIA). It happens when the brain experiences the loss of oxygen for a short time due to insufficient blood supply caused by a clot or a small plaque. A clot or plaque occludes blood flow to the brain transiently without having a lasting effect in TIA. It is technically not a stroke because the symptoms disappear within minutes to an hour. Brain cells are not damaged permanently but it is a warning sign that a full stroke may occur in the future. However, if the symptoms do not disappear within twenty-four hours, it is considered a full stroke.

About fifteen percent of patients who have suffered a TIA have a full stroke within three months. A TIA is very similar to an ischemic stroke. The victim may suffer from weakness of the body, confusion, slurred speech, eyesight problems, difficulty in walking, dizziness, and imbalance. A drug like aspirin prevents clot formation and is recommended for patients at risk of having TIA. They should also avoid cigarette smoking and alcohol intake that can potentially cause heart diseases or high blood pressure. Those with diabetes are advised to keep their sugar in check.

It is important to understand that the drugs used for the treatment of ischemic and hemorrhagic strokes are completely different. In the case of the former, the focus is on opening up the blood vessels, while in the latter, immediate attention is on stopping the bleeding. Therefore, the drug aspirin that is used as a blood thinner was not suitable for me, even though in the case of an ischemic stroke patient, this might be the first line of treatment. Cholesterol-lowering drugs like statin or anti-clotting drugs such as Warfarin may also be used in patients of ischemic stroke, especially those who are obese or prone to arterial fibrillation. My doctors decided that, for me, rehabilitation through various therapies was the best course for my recovery from the stroke.

There can be many underlying causes of a stroke. These include, but are not restricted to, high blood pressure, stress, diabetes, heart problems, obesity, substance abuse, or smoking. So why did I fall victim to this debilitating medical emergency?

I found out later that my stroke was due to a congenital arteriovenous malformation (AVM). An AVM is a kind of vascular anomaly that develops when an artery is directly connected to a vein, without developing the normal capillary network. This disrupts normal blood flow and oxygen circulation. Though AVMs can occur in any part of the body, they most often occur in the brain or spinal cord. In some cases, AVMs can cause bleeding, intense pain, and many other problems. This is why hemorrhagic strokes are sometimes associated with intense headaches or epileptic seizures though, in a majority of cases, people suffering from AVM are asymptomatic. I was fortunate in this regard because I did not suffer from these symptoms. My headaches before the stroke were restricted to about once a month. Now, after the stroke, I rarely ever get headaches.

Scientists still are undecided about whether or not to treat AVMs. The treatment involves surgery, radiation, drugs, or a combination of all these. While these methods have many benefits, they are not devoid of risks and side-effects. As it was in my case, sometimes it is safer to avoid surgery altogether and cope with the dangers of an AVM. An alternative to surgery is to opt for gamma knife radiation therapy, which is a procedure to make blood vessels stronger. I was advised to undergo this form of treatment by my doctors.

My neurosurgeon later informed me that because my AVM was a kind of birth defect and the stroke inevitable. It could have very well happened when I was ten years old! I was lucky to have evaded it all these years. In retrospect, what if the cerebral hemorrhage had happened when I was in the restroom—alone and unattended. Or worse, while driving. The stroke could have led to a devastating road accident, which could have not only cost me my life, but also that of others. The what-ifs are endless. And I can only be grateful that it happened when it did—neither sooner nor later. Had the stroke happened just two weeks hence, I would have been stranded in South Africa—a foreign country, possibly without access to the kind of medical aid and facility I received in the United States. Instead, it happened when I was sitting comfortably in my office chair, talking over the phone with a student from my pharmacology class.

3

BEGINNING OF MY BATTLES

21 October. Dodd Hall, OSU Rehabilitation Hospital

I opened my eyes slowly as if in a daze. A bright, white ceiling greeted me. *Where was I?* My thoughts as confused as my hazy vision, it slowly dawned upon me that I was in a hospital. *A hospital? Why am I in a hospital?*

When I woke up for the first time that day, I was still groggy and under the influence of a dream I had. It was a frightening dream in which I had been wrongly admitted to the OSU Hospital in Jeffersonville, Ohio. Unable to differentiate my dream from reality, I recall asking my wife Sarla when our neighbor, Mr. Beant Nindra, would visit me. My plan was to secretly escape from the hospital with Mr. Nindra! Unfortunately, that was not to happen. Mr. Nindra was in Malaysia at the time. By the time he came to visit me, I comprehended that I had suffered a massive hemorrhagic stroke.

I recall the first Saturday after I was moved to Dodd Hall. The date was October 25. Ohio State Buckeyes versus Penn State Nittany Lions football game was on TV. My son Samir was by my side watching the game, but I was so weak and drowsy that I could not follow the game as I usually did.

My initial days at Dodd Hall went by in a blur. While some conversations and occurrences during those days, such as the football match, remain with me, other memories are hazy. I learned later that I was shifted to Dodd Hall two weeks after I suffered the stroke. Slowly and steadily, I started understanding what had happened to me on that fateful day. I believe it was my former post postdoctoral fellow, Ravinder, who broke the news to me in the hospital.

"Dr. Tejwani, do you know that you suffered from an AVM?"

I knew what an AVM was. Arteriovenous Malformation.

Ravinder's words were still ringing in my ears when that all-pervading question assaulted me. *Why me?* This question haunted me for a long time and it took months of therapy and assistance before I could accept it as my new reality.

Why did I suffer from an AVM? Why was there so much bleeding in my brain? I was healthy before my stroke. I exercised at least four times a week and did not suffer from other medical conditions like hypertension, diabetes, hypercholesterolemia (elevated blood level of cholesterol), or obesity, which are considered risk factors for a stroke. Not surprisingly, my initial reaction was that it was the end of my life. I was not mentally ready to cope with the aftermath of a life-threatening stroke. My fragile state of mind at the time even led me to believe that somehow the stroke was the result of my doing. Even when I was released from the OSU hospital after six weeks of hospitalization, I couldn't shake away the "why me?" question.

After Ravinder informed me of my AVM, I began to slowly recall the day of the stroke. My last memory was of the office when I was speaking to my student on phone. The events of the following hours and days were filled in by family and friends.

On realizing that something was not right, my student from the pharmacology class rushed to my department and met our secretary Cheryl, who then rushed to my office where she found me unconscious and lying in a pool of vomit. My lunchbox was still open with my half-eaten lunch inside. She immediately called paramedics who were working at the OSU College of Medicine Hospital, a block away from my office. I have a vague and transient recollection of events when the paramedics came.

I remember lying on the floor as a paramedic in a white uniform cleaned the vomit from my shirt. He also asked me if I was okay. I have no recollection of my reply if any. Meanwhile, Cheryl called up Sarla to tell get her up to speed on the events of the day. Sarla rushed to my office, and on the way broke the news to Samir, an orthopedic surgeon working in California, and many of my friends. Samir came to Columbus on the same day.

Paramedics had taken me to the OSU hospital around 2 pm. At the hospital, doctors had a hard time diagnosing my problem. It took them about four hours to ascertain that I had a hemorrhagic stroke. Since I had vomited, and my lunch box was still open when the paramedics came, doctors initially suspected a case of food poisoning. They then checked my medical records to see if I had any issues involving blood pressure or congestive heart failure. However, my records were clear of any underlying medical conditions. After ruling out food poisoning and a cardiovascular anomaly, I was checked for cerebral issues. At around 6 pm, a brain Magnetic Resonance Imaging (MRI) was done, which showed an AVM or a ruptured vein in the medulla close to my vascular and respiratory nuclei.

In all this chaos, Samir had the additional task of locating my car in the OSU garage. He told me later that he searched for my car on each floor, east and west side, of a six-story garage! He also cleared the penalty to the Chicago police that I had attempted to pay earlier in the day.

An AVM can occur in any part of the body. In my case, it happened in the brain. It occurs when arteries join directly with veins without a meshwork of connecting capillaries. AVMs can cause pain, bleeding, or other problems of venous (impure) blood getting mixed with arterial (pure) blood. In some cases, a patient may have no symptoms at all. Unfortunately, the AVM in my brain caused considerable bleeding in my brain stem in the medulla region.

The question remained as to what caused my AVM in the first place. Sarla and Samir were informed that mine seemed to be a congenital problem and not associated with any particular disease in the body. Typically, treatment for AVMs is symptomatic. Patients are monitored closely for epileptic seizures, headaches, or other neurologic problems. Surgery is the treatment of choice in many cases. In my case, however, this was not an option. My neurosurgeon ruled out surgery because my AVM was in the pontine nuclei in my brain stem, close to the cardiovascular and respiratory nuclei. Surgery was deemed too risky as a miscalculation by the neurosurgeon could leave me blind, or worse, dead. As an alternative, I was kept on a drug-induced coma for a few days to decrease the workload on my brain. I was put on oxygen support and left to heal by myself. After a few days when doctors observed that I could breathe on my own, the oxygen supplement was stopped. However, doctors informed my family that there was nothing more to be done. I was now at the mercy of God. If I recovered, well and good, otherwise it was the end of the road of me.

I have a fuzzy recollection of what took place in the first two weeks when I was in a coma. I remember some of my dreams from this time. I also have a vague recollection of a conversation I had with one of my ex-students, Dr. Kuldeep Vaswani. I pleaded with him to remove the feeding tube from my abdomen. Naturally, he refused. I also remember speaking to my wife's cousin, Jaggu, who flew in from Atlanta to see me. Jaggu would often ask me in Sindhi, *"Sai kahido hall ahe?"* [Sir, how are you?].

Sarla told me later that the news of my passing out and being admitted to the ICU spread like wildfire in Columbus. Many of my friends came to visit me that very day though they were not allowed in the ICU at the time. Even so, dozens of friends and well-wishers visited every day. She jokes that after a few days of this, the information officer at the hospital desk simply revealed my hospital room number to any Indian who visited the OSU Hospital, presuming that they had all come to see me! In fact, a *pundit* (Hindu priest) from the Bhartiya Hindu Temple and a *gyani* (a Sikh priest) from local Gurdwara (a Sikh temple) also came to offer their prayers for me and wish me a speedy recovery.

Since I was in a coma in the ICU, one of the problems faced by my doctors was to find means to feed me.

There were two ways to do this. My doctors discussed both options with my son, a doctor himself. The first procedure involved drilling a hole in my neck and esophagus and insert a feeding tube from there. The other was to insert a feeding tube—in medical terms, this is called a PEG (Percutaneous Endoscopic Gastrostomy) tube—directly into my stomach through a hole in my abdomen. My son preferred the latter. The PEG tube was inserted on October 16, 2008. When I emerged from my coma, I found a tube hanging from my abdomen. This feeding tube was connected with a bag that was used to deliver a semi-solid meal of about 1,700 calories. I don't know what kind of meal it was, but it was mushy and orange in color.

Though I was in a coma, it seems I attempted escaping from the hospital several times. As a result, I was restrained and was kept on watch day and night. In retrospect, my attempt at running away from the hospital might be because of a recurring dream I had while in the ICU. In fact, I recall many of my dreams from this time. They were all disturbing.

Before my stroke, my wife and I would often go to Tanger Outlet Mall in Jeffersonville, Ohio. In my dream, I saw my wife and I leaving the mall after we were done with our shopping. But before we could leave, we were arrested by the security of the newly established OSU-run hospital in Jeffersonville. I soon realized that this was because the OSU hospital was new in the area and desperate for new patients! We were their victims! After our arrest, I was taken to the hospital and was forced to wear a chastity belt-like device prohibiting me from urinating. As a result, I developed a urinary infection. To top this atrocity, the doctors at this hospital demanded 600 pesos (about $200 in my dream) to treat me. Very reluctantly, I parted with this sum so I could be treated and both Sarla and I were released from the hospital. As bizarre as this dream was, what is stranger is the knowledge that I, in fact, did have a urinary infection during the time I was at the OSU ICU. The only difference being that my doctors did not, of course, hold me hostage, and I was successfully treated with the help of antibiotics.

However, at the time of my coma, my dreams were my reality. I did not know any better. The indignity of being arrested in OSU made me furious and I had thought to myself how could OSU arrest its faculty member! Just for a few hundred dollars? It was preposterous. To remedy this injustice, I dreamt that after returning to my OSU office, I wrote a long letter to the then-president of OSU, Gordon Gee, demanding back all the money I paid to the OSU after my arrest in Jeffersonville. Justice was served. I was returned my money and offered an apology claiming that they were not aware of the fact that I was an OSU employee.

Thinking back on my dream, I now realize that it may have had a direct impact on my thinking and behavior at the time. This is the reason that after waking from the coma, I used to ask my wife about my friend and neighbor, Mr. Nindra. The plan was to escape from the hospital with him as I was convinced that I had no health issues and was kept there under false pretexts.

Another peculiar dream I had was about Dr. Rebekah Gee and her husband. In July 2008, the OSU president Gordon Gee's newly married daughter Dr. Rebekah Gee and her husband, Dr. Allan Moore, were seriously injured in a scooter accident in Philadelphia. This was about three months before my stroke. Sadly, Dr. Moore did not make it and succumbed to his injuries. Even though I had met President Gee on many occasions, I had neither met his daughter Rebekah nor her late husband. However, the incident must have left a deep impact on my subconscious—something I did not realize at the time. When in my coma, I dreamt of a sobbing Rebekah waiting outside the ICU eager to know of her husband's fate. In the dream, I tried to console the deeply anguished woman, assuring her that her husband would be fine. I also saw the critically injured Dr. More being attended to by doctors. I was deeply saddened by the events. Thinking back, I can't fathom why I had this dream; except possibly the fact that the news of this accident had deeply disturbed me in my waking state.

In another one of my dreams, I was a student in a caricature-drawing class at the OSU. This was a frustrating dream in which I was constantly given new caricatures to draw even though I had successfully completed the previous ones. Each new sketch I had to draw came with a frightening caveat that if I wanted to live, I had to complete the sketch. To make things worse, I was repeatedly given a C grade, despite my best efforts at doing a good job. I recall two more dreams about the OSU. In one of them, my blood samples were being analyzed in a clinical chemistry laboratory by technicians of Somali origin. In another, I was the chairperson of the Department of Statistics, and was merry-making with my female graduate students of Indian origin!

Yet another peculiar dream I had involved members of a religious cult called Heaven's Gate. I have no idea why I had this dream since I have no connections with this cult or any of its members or leaders. However, this cult exists, and news reports on it may have stayed on in my subconscious. In 1997, thirty-nine young people (21 women and 18 men) committed mass suicide in matching dark clothes and Nike sneakers in Ranch Santa Fe, a suburb of San Diego. They all were members of Heaven's Gate. It is said that leaders of the cult preached to members that suicide will allow them to leave their bodily "containers" and enter an alien spacecraft hidden behind the Hale-Bopp comet. In my dream, I saw the members of this cult. They were lying dead on the floor.

I don't know the significance of all these dreams except, perhaps, the dream about the drawing class. Looking back, the dream was symbolic at many levels. Perhaps, it was a sign that I needed to keep trying, and never give up. In my dream, I had to keep drawing the caricatures if I wanted to live—it was hard work, even in a dream. I realize today that life has become nothing but hard work. Repetitious tasks are essential to overcome the debilitating effects of a stroke. Post-stroke therapy involves a lot of repetitious work, but this is essential as it helps the patient live independently. Hard work pays dividends to a stroke patient and helps improve the quality of life. Therefore, I urge all victims of stroke not to give up and be patient and persistent.

I was probably in the ICU when my wife was told that the right side of my body, including my leg and arm, was paralyzed. This is known as hemiplegia, and it was an aftereffect of the stroke. At that time, I did not know that the stroke would partially paralyze my body and weaken my limbs. When I finally gained consciousness at Dodd Hall, I could not touch the fingers of my right hand with the thumb and could barely move my right arm or right leg. I couldn't stand on my own and was wheelchair-bound for three months. When I talked—though it made perfect sense to me—my speech garbled. My friends later told me that it was difficult for them to comprehend what I was saying at the time.

It was an uphill task for me to relearn many common chores, such as brushing my teeth, taking a bath, putting on my clothes, or tying shoelaces. To this day, my right leg remains weak. It has been a constant struggle. It required hard work, determination, family support, and consistent effort on my part to see any improvement. My optimism and never-say-die attitude have helped me overcome many of my limitations and led me to where I am today.

4

A PATH LAID WITH THORNS

A mountain as high as the sky stood ahead of me. Emerging from the coma was just a tiny step up. The rocky path ahead was yet to begin. I realized quickly that I had to face numerous setbacks before my life could even begin to resemble what it had been like before.

When I woke up in the Rehabilitation Hospital, I noticed two things. First, a plastic tube was hanging from my stomach. This was my food bag. Since I was in a coma for two weeks, my body was getting the nutrition it needed through this tube, which was inserted directly into my stomach. The second was that a nurse would drain my urinary bladder by inserting a catheter through my urethra. This process was done a few times a day.

The stroke had made my muscles weak, especially on the right side of my body and urinary bladder. I could not urinate on my own. Without external help, there was a possibility that my bladder would explode or rupture due to the pressure built up inside. The nurse used to bring an instrument and measure the accumulated urine volume in my bladder. When it was about 600–700 ml, she would insert a catheter and drain the liquid by gently pressing my abdomen. However, she noticed that there was always a residual urine volume of about 150 ml that could not be drained. To remedy this, my doctor prescribed tamsulosin hydrochloride (sold under the trade name Flomax). This is a medicine used to improve urine flow in men, especially those suffering from an enlarged prostate. An enlarged prostate gland constricts urinary muscles in the urethra, thus inhibiting urine flow. Flomax is used to relax the surrounding muscles ensuring greater urine outflow. I am not aware if this medication helped me, but as soon as I was released from the hospital, I stopped taking Flomax, afraid that I would become completely dependent on Flomax for the rest of my life.

I clearly remember the nurse encouraging me to urinate on my own. She would often run water through a tap in the sink. She would make me listen to the sound of the water stream and encourage me to urinate but it did not work. Finally, one day out of sheer frustration she told me that every time she uses the kit containing a catheter to drain my urine, the hospital was billed a whopping $600!

This was in the second week of November, days before my discharge on November 15. By this time, I had spent more than five weeks in the hospital. The thought of going home without acquiring the ability to urinate on my own petrified me! *How would I manage?* This thought started to haunt me, more so because my right hand was too weak to be of any use. I knew I could not insert a catheter on my own and my wife knew nothing about this process either. *Do I have to call a nurse home every day? Not once or twice, maybe even three times or more! Who will bear the expenditure?* These thoughts plagued me, so I spoke with my doctor and social worker to permit me to stay for a few more days in the hospital. Luckily for me, the insurance company relented and I was permitted to stay for five more days in the hospital.

With the news of the extension coming in, I was relieved and also determined to urinate on my own. Every day, I would run a tap to listen to the sound of running water and encourage myself to urinate. For three days, nothing happened. On the fourth day, two days before my release from the hospital, a small miracle happened. I could finally urinate on my own! I was ecstatic. I would have never imagined that a simple act of urinating on my own could give me such a sense of achievement. Life is strange, indeed.

Today, I have no problems with urination at all though once in a while, I need to wake up in the middle of the night to do this. But then again, at seventy-plus, this is normal. Speaking of nights, there is something else that bothers me now and then, even though when I was at the hospital, this was taken care of—sleeplessness.

When I was in the hospital, I was given a melatonin tablet for sleep. Melatonin is a naturally produced hormone synthesized in the pineal gland in the brain. It is involved in the regulation of sleep and wake-up cycles in the body. It is considered a good natural treatment for people having difficulty with sleep after air travel. However, after being on Melatonin for a few days, I realized that I had a sound sleep for three to four hours, after which I would be unable to sleep. Since I was given the medicine at about 9:30 pm, I spend a large part of the night, awake, staring up at the ceiling! Very soon, this oddity started bothering me and I discussed it with my attending physician. My medication was switched to Trazodone, a drug that is typically used to treat depression but also prescribed for treating insomnia. Trazodone induced sleep but left its mark throughout the day. Once a physician-friend who was visiting during a therapy class observed that it was difficult for me to keep my eyes open during my sessions. He was correct. Trazodone was working a little *too* well for me!

Once again, I had a chat with my attending physician and I was prescribed Ritalin in addition to Trazodone. Ritalin is a stimulant belonging to a class of amphetamine-type drugs generally prescribed for ADHD. So, I was given a Trazodone tablet at night to induce sleep and then a Ritalin tablet in the morning to keep me alert throughout the day. This routine went on for a few days.

Being a pharmacologist by profession, I did not want to get hooked onto either drug. So once again, I discussed my problem with the attending physician and convinced him to not prescribe Ritalin. I was okay being drowsy during the day but the thought of getting addicted to these drugs was not appealing. I continued taking Trazodone for some more time. My insomnia problem remains to this day. After returning home, I took a different drug, Lunesta, for a while. But stopped eventually. There are too many stories of people (celebrities included) getting hooked onto sleeping pills, and I did not want to be one of them. Develop tolerance or dependence on any of these medications was not an option for me so I finally resorted to Melatonin, which is a natural hormone with fewer side-effects if any. I have not had much success with my insomnia, and I accept it as one of the ill-effects of the stroke I must live with.

I often wondered why my sleeping pattern was deranged after the stroke, so I read up as much as I could on the subject. The answer lies in a small thumb-sized organ in the brain stem called the pons. This organ is critical for relaying messages from the cortex and the cerebellum and is responsible for regulating the sleep cycle of an individual as well as controlling respiration. It also plays a key role in sleep and dreaming. Since my stroke occurred in the brain stem, it affected the pons. Rapid Eye Movement (REM) sleep that is associated with deep sleep (a sleeping state when most dreams occur) is linked to the pons. So any damage to the pontine area would disturb my sleep forever until the time my body can repair the pons. How many neurons were killed in the pontine area, no one can say with certainty. However, some certainly did, which resulted in my disturbed sleep cycle. This, in addition to restricted physical activity, made things worse.

With my weak right side, I was hardly able to do routine work, let aside any hard physical work. Since I cannot repair the damage to my pontine area affected by the stroke, I decided to incorporate more physical exercise in my daily life. Before the stroke, I exercised regularly—I used to walk about three times a week, in addition to other household activities requiring modest exertion such as mowing my lawn, and so on. I have now started walking regularly again for one hour a day in my neighborhood. Rain or shine, winter or summer, I am on the road. If at all this is impossible because of bad weather, I walk indoors going from one room to another!

This mild exercise is sufficient to induce about six hours of sleep without any medication. The day I walk more—at times my wife and I visit a mall nearby—I can sleep for an hour or two more. I find that the odd day when I am unable to walk for some reason, I have trouble sleeping. This happens about once a week only. On such days, I take a tablet of Tylenol PM and can get good seven hours of sleep.

Tackling a lack of sleep in elderly people

Sleeplessness or insomnia is a common old-age issue. While this can be exaggerated due to other underlying medical conditions, like the stroke in my case, there are some simple tips and tricks that can help ameliorate this problem. I list a few that I find useful.

Chant a word

Chanting a word or a short phrase can help induce sleep naturally. My favorite chanting words include "Wahe Guru," "Sat Nam," "Hare Ram," and "Jesus."

Count numbers

Sometimes forward or backward counting is a good technique to induce sleep. If you are having trouble sleeping, try counting 1, 2, 3, 4 ... 100 or 100, 99, 98,

97 … 0. Many a time, I have fallen asleep even before reaching the target—100 or 0.

Free your mind

I find that a clear mind free of worry does wonder. Do not worry about things beyond your control. What you can control, you must do, but bedtime is not the time to organize those thoughts. Also, keeping away your gadgets, especially your cell phone, is very important. My cell phone and I are never in the same room at night!

Stop looking at the clock

Looking at the clock repeatedly when you are unable to sleep serves no purpose. In my experience, when I did *not* see the clock, I was able to go back to sleep for some time.

Get out of bed

This solution might not work for everyone, especially those who have a day job to go to. But if you are retired like me, I suggest that you get out of bed if your sleep is broken very early in the morning at about 5 am or so. Watch some TV, read a newspaper or magazine or simply get on with your daily chores. By doing this, you might start feeling sleepy again in two or three hours, and if that is the case, feel free to take a nap.

Lower the ambient nighttime temperature

Keeping a slightly lower room temperature at night can aid sleep. A four-degree drop in temperature can do wonders. For example, if you are used to a daytime temperature of 72 degrees Fahrenheit (22 ºC), then lowering to temperature to 68 degrees Fahrenheit (20 ºC) can be helpful. You can always use a light blanket to cover yourself.

Deep breathing

Practice deep breathing to calm your mind. Many respiratory experts recommend the 4-4-4 rule—take a deep breath for four seconds, hold the breath for another four seconds, and exhale breath for another four seconds. Some others recommend the 4-7-8 seconds inhale-hold-exhale cycle. However, deep breathing techniques require practice and are not quick-fix solutions. A good starting point can be trying out a partial (or modified) breathing technique, based on what is comfortable to you.

Maintain a sleeping schedule

Many sleeping experts recommend following a strict sleeping schedule. The body likes to take rest at the same time every day, so try to sleep at a fixed time every day. I sleep at about 11 pm every day.

Avoid caffeine before bedtime

Caffeine is a central nervous system stimulant. Drinking coffee (or other caffeine-rich products like tea) 6–12 hours before bedtime can disturb your sleep. I am a tea drinker but my second and last cup of tea is usually at 4 pm—seven hours before I sleep. While it is okay to consume decaffeinated drinks, remember this doesn't rid them of their diuretic properties.

Restrict water intake before sleep

Many elderly people need to use the bathroom frequently at night. This problem can be resolved by restricting large amounts of fluid intake before going to bed. Since I go to bed at 11 pm, I try to avoid drinking water after 7:30 pm.

Avoid alcoholic drinks

Alcoholic drinks should be strictly avoided by anyone having insomnia issues. Alcohol shortens sleep time; it is a diuretic, and also makes one thirsty. All these can lead to a disturbed sleeping pattern. It is; therefore, best to avoid alcoholic drinks 6 to 12 hours before bedtime.

Exercise regularly

I find that daily exercise is the best cure for insomnia. This is true for most stroke victims. Those with weak limbs can do gentle exercises. The most effective exercise I find is walking for about an hour daily. I sleep even better on days that I get 90 minutes of walking. But it is a good idea to exercise 4–6 hours before bedtime.

One of the numerous problems I faced in the Rehabilitation Hospital was that of double vision— in medical terms, diplopia. My hospital room had a framed painting hanging on the wall. It was the first thing I saw every morning. But it took me a while to realize there was just, not two paintings. It seemed to me as if they were superimposed on each other. I often wondered why this was so. Why hang two paintings on the wall and superimpose them on one another? The same was true for the TV set! Very soon I realized that I was seeing double images even though I had no double vision issues when seeing people. In my case, the stroke affected the left side of the brain, making most of the muscles on the right side of my body weak. This included the muscles of my right eye. Because of this, I was not able to clearly see the painting on the wall or watch television properly.

Let me give you an example. In the early days after being shifted to the rehabilitation hospital, I was watching a football game on the television with my son. The OSU against Penn State. But for me, the manner in which the defensive players were tackling offensive players was very intriguing. It seemed to be that the defensive players were moving very rapidly—almost flying—to be near the offense players!

This was because my stroke occurred in the brain stem and destroyed my cerebellum, which in addition to affecting my movement also affected my vision. To see properly, muscles in both eyes must be healthy and coordinate properly. In my case, the muscles in the right eye had become weak causing the double vision problem. When I discussed the problem with my doctor, he readily referred me to the OSU Department of Ophthalmology. After a thorough examination of my eyes, the ophthalmologist wrote me a prescription for new glasses. My new prescription glasses had a prism that helped produce a single vision and enabled me to see normally. Thankfully, my double vision problem has not bothered me since then.

Eyesight problems following a stroke

To understand visual difficulties after a stroke, it is important to first understand how eyes, nerves, and the brain coordinate to produce a perfect image for us to see and how the stroke affects this coordination.

Nerves relay images from the eyes to the brain where these images are processed and interpreted in the occipital area of the brain for us to see a perfect picture. The eye muscles help us coordinate what we see, and this information is stored in our temporary memory allowing the brain to help us move perfectly. For example, when walking down a staircase, the eyes send this information to the brain which then decides how much each foot must move down so that we take a safe and calculated step. If this coordination is skewed, we can miss a step and fall. Both eyes must coordinate properly to produce a perfect picture.

When I was recovering in the OSU Rehabilitation Hospital in Dodd Hall, I used to go for physical or occupational therapy every day. The latter was not very strenuous and mainly involved sharpening existing skills necessary for my occupation. Physical therapy, however, was strenuous for me, especially because I could hardly stand on my own at the time and was confined to a wheelchair.

Physical therapy involved moving leg and hand muscles and put sufficient workload on the heart—enough to raise my heart rate dramatically. One day, the doctor measured my heart rate after about thirty minutes of therapy. It was at 130 instead of returning to a normal heart rate of about 72 beats per minute. This was alarming and he immediately considered the worst possible scenario—a blood clot in my lungs! He surmised that a blood clot from my legs could travel to my pulmonary artery in the lungs leading to a pulmonary embolism at any time. That would explain my increased heart rate thirty minutes after therapy. This was around 8 pm. He immediately notified my wife who had reached home after spending the day with me at the hospital. The poor thing had to return to the hospital again as I rushed to a different building for an MRI. At 9 pm, I was wheeled into the radiology department. I had to remove all my jewelry and most of my clothes to get in a coffin-shaped box. There was no room to move at all. The process took about thirty minutes to complete. The result was positive—no clot in my lungs! I was thankful and my wife went back home relieved.

The next day, my doctor prescribed Metoprolol, a beta-blocker meant to slow down the heart rate and also decrease blood pressure. I have been taking Metoprolol faithfully for twelve years now. The question, however, remained: if the elevation in my heart rate was not due to the presence of a blood clot in the lungs then what caused it? My doctor never gave me an explanation. Months after my discharge from the hospital, I got my answer after a thorough literature survey of my own.

My stroke occurred in the brain stem which is located just below the limbic system controlling our emotions. The brain stem is responsible for sustaining essential functions of life such as respiration, heartbeat, and blood pressure. It consists of the midbrain, pons, and medulla. The medulla is involved in controlling breathing, swallowing, and heart rate. It is a vital organ present between the brain and the spinal cord. The hemorrhage that occurred in the brain stem during my stroke must have destroyed certain neurons in the medulla resulting in the disturbance of my heartbeat.

I learned that a stroke can produce not only locomotive problems in the limbs but many problems associated with various muscles and areas of the brain. One can never be sure about what kind of medical problem may crop up in the future but these are beyond our control. What we can do is to prepare our mind for facing any eventuality. No matter in what shape one is, it is important to remember that millions in this world are worse off. Always thank the Almighty for all the good that remains.

5

HOMECOMING

November 20. After forty-two days at the hospital, it was time to go home.

But before this could happen, a lot was going on behind the scenes. My house was being readied to accommodate my special needs. According to the American Disability Act of the 1980s, hospital staff is required to determine whether or not a house is fit to accommodate a disabled person. For this, they must pay a visit to the house to check if everything is in place. This was done in my case as well. The hospital staff including most of the therapy staff as well as a social worker visited my home to check for everything. They had given us a couple of weeks to get the work done. The bathrooms needed proper grab bars so that when I get up from the toilet seat, I had something to hold onto; the stairs needed fixed hand railings for support; a wheelchair ramp was required at the front of the house, and so on. Since many homes are not constructed for wheelchair-bound people, they need to make sure that the entrance to the home clears the wheelchair. All this is done so that a disabled person is as independent as possible and can enter and exit the home safely, and in case of an emergency, he/she does not have to struggle unnecessarily.

The main door of our house was wide enough for a wheelchair but the small stoop needed a ramp to be built over it. I was worried as to who would do this job, especially since my wife has no experience in this regard and my right hand was incapacitated. Fortunately, my friends offered to help. One of them who is an engineer got some help from his company and built a ramp at the entrance of my house. Another one installed the grab bars in the bathroom and a handrail in the garage.

On the day of my homecoming, a friend gave me a ride back home in her car. The wheelchair was folded and placed in the trunk and reassembled on reaching home. When my wife tried to push the wheelchair over the newly built ramp, she couldn't! The ramp was built a little too high for her. As a result, my friend had to help out as well. This naturally worried me. *How will I and Sarla manage without outside help?*

Luckily, life offers solutions most of the time. We got around this seemingly big hurdle by using the garage entrance to the house. And so it was settled. I would use the garage door to enter and exit the house. The only pitfall was that the time and effort spent in building the ramp was a total waste!

Once inside, there was another predicament facing us. We had no bedrooms on the ground floor, and at the time, it was not possible for me to climb stairs to the bedroom on the first floor. Yet again, my friends came to my rescue. They brought my bed from the bedroom to the family room downstairs to create a temporary bedroom downstairs. But a bigger problem was the lack of a bathroom on the ground floor. All the showers were upstairs! There was only a toilet downstairs but where would I take a shower?

Luckily, a close family friend, Mona Advani, had a great suggestion—a temporary bathroom. Her mother-in-law had suffered a stroke in the past, and she had experience in taking care of stroke victims. We decided to heed her advice. Promptly, she visited Lowes and purchased a temporary bathroom that could be assembled at home and attached to normal plumbing. A hired mechanic did this job for us.

The new bathroom was barely a little larger than a normal-sized refrigerator and without a front door or curtain for privacy. This might seem awkward but since stroke patients, like me, are dependent on others for showering, it was not a deal-breaker. At that time, I still had the feeding tube attached to my abdomen even though I was eating orally. So I had to be extra careful about this while taking a shower.

It took me about six months to recuperate at home. In all my years at the OSU, I had not taken a single sick leave. As a result, I had accumulated more than two years of sick leave that came in handy at the time.

My recovery came in incremental steps. The first was, of course, gaining strength through exercise and therapy. A few weeks after returning home, I was also permitted to remove the feeding tube from my stomach. This procedure took place at the hospital. Later on, I also underwent gamma knife surgery. During all stages, my wife was a pillar of strength for me. She stood beside me like a rock, never faltering, never wavering, from the day of my stroke up until now.

6

A SLOW ROAD TO RECOVERY

My wife was the biggest supporter and reassurance for me in the hospital. Every morning at seven-thirty, she would be by my side. My life at the Rehabilitation Hospital was challenging to say the least. Not only was I struggling to cope with the physical disabilities brought about by the stroke, but I was also in a fragile state of mind. With consciousness came the question— why me? There was also a sense of despondency that had taken hold of me. From a healthy active individual, I was now unable to do the simplest and most mundane of self-care activities, such as brushing my teeth or urinating on my own. I was dependent on others for everything. The only thing I knew was that I had to fight, and fight hard—harder than ever before. Success came in small, at times infinitesimal steps, but they were, nevertheless, steps forward, and I trudged on.

During my first two weeks here, I was fed using a feeding tube attached to my stomach through my abdomen. Naturally, I did not like this and wanted it removed at the earliest. On November 4, 2008, the hospital scheduled a Fiberoptic Endoscopic Evaluation of Swallowing (FEES) to check whether the food ingested from the mouth was directly entering the stomach, or in case of a swallowing disorder, entering the windpipe. This test would also identify the safest foods for me. The FEES was done by a Speech Language Pathologist (SLP).

For the test, the SLP offered me bagel and cheese along with a glass of juice. A bagel is considered tough to ingest so if I could eat this, I could probably have anything! A large machine was attached to me to monitor my food intake. The sandwich and juice had barium in it, so its passage through my body could be monitored on the screen. I was allowed to take normal bites. Luckily, I passed the test with flying colors and was permitted to eat solid food. Finally, after four weeks, I could eat solid food again. It was a big step forward in my recovery journey. Most of the time, I would have a breakfast of a French toast and a turkey sandwich and fruit for lunch. For dinner, my friends would bring me home-cooked Indian food, which I relished with great enthusiasm.

Recovery meant a host of rigorous therapy sessions that were all focused on enabling me to live my life as independently as possible. But my therapy could not start immediately after I came home. It was late November and with the Thanksgiving and Christmas holidays coming up, I was informed by the hospital that the department was not scheduling any new sessions till December end. As a result, I had to wait for almost five weeks before commencing therapy. I was scheduled for two therapy sessions per week. At that time, I had no idea that my therapy sessions would have to continue for at least two years! I was to have physical, occupational, and cognitive therapy.

The physical therapy was to improve my strength, mobility, and fitness. Since I had not done any physical activity since my release from the hospital, physical therapy was very taxing. I remember, when I first went to the physical therapy session in my wheelchair, three people had to help me to stand on my own and walk about twenty feet. In fact, on the first day of therapy at Martha More House, I blacked out from exhaustion! My blood pressure had suddenly fallen for some reason. Thankfully, after about fifteen minutes of rest, I was okay. At another time, my heartbeat increased to more than 130 beats per minute! I was rushed for an MRI of the lungs to rule out any blood clots that could potentially cause a pulmonary embolism. Emboli can also cause heart attacks.

In my two years of physical therapy, the focus was on strengthening my muscles. I was made to lift weights, walk (initially with support from therapists), lift articles from the floor, and move my body in different ways. When I first started using the treadmill, my body was supported by several body belts to prevent me from collapsing. Later on, I graduated to brisk walking on the treadmill, using an exercise bike, and stretching exercises using resistance bands.

One of the things I asked my therapist was how to get up from the floor in case of a fall. He told me that I should do this by first placing my left hand on the floor to partially raise myself, then stand up straight using the help of an immovable object like a sofa or a bed.

Occupational therapy was meant to help me cope with daily life, such as how to change my clothes and socks, tie my shoelaces, and so on. Since the right side of my body was weak from the stroke, the focus of therapy was to restore strength and finer movements of my right hand. I was given all sorts of activities such as using nuts and bolts, screwdrivers, and various other hand exercises, all designed to strengthen the muscles of my right hand. Even though I did not have to use physical strength for these exercises, they were hard to do. Even after six weeks of therapy, I could not perfect any of the activities, especially wearing socks and tying my shoelaces. Little did I know at that time that it would take me another eight years of practice to gain sufficient strength to tie shoelaces on my own! For anyone else in a similar predicament, I will only suggest that do not allow yourself to be demotivated. It is a good idea to keep practicing these activities at home too because repeating therapy lessons at home accelerates the return of strength in your body and brings back normalcy to your life.

While I struggled with my physical and occupational therapy classes, my cognitive therapy sessions were a great success right from the start. This meant that my memory and thought process was normal despite the stroke. I was made to do backward counting, map reading, and solve mind games and simple calculations. I was given articles to read and then summarize their content. This was to assess my comprehension skills. I excelled at all these exercises and hospital therapists were rather impressed by my performance! At the end of my therapy, I had to give a lecture in pharmacology to the therapy staff to convince them that I was still capable of returning to the OSU to teach.

When I was recuperating from the stroke, a podiatrist friend of mine suggested using an electrical machine to stimulate the muscles of my right leg. He suggested that stimulation therapy may be able to generate new nerves or reactivate the old nerves in the brain, which in turn might restore strength and dexterity in my right hand and leg. His clinic was fifteen miles from my home. Since I could not drive at the time, I informed him that it would be difficult for me to commute this large distance. On hearing this, he even offered to lend me the machine and to keep at home for as long as I needed to. But I was not aware of the value of stimulation therapy at that time, so I politely declined his offer. It was much later when I visited India that I first experienced electrical stimulation of my right leg and foot. This was at a private clinic where I used to go for physical therapy. I faithfully took the fifteen-minute stimulation sessions for two months during my time in the country. Also, the cost factor is worth mentioning. The price of a one-hour-session involving multiple instruments, stimulation therapy, and helpers was only a dollar in India compared to about seventy-five in the United States. Having said that, there was, of course, a difference in the quality of therapy. In the United States, therapists are highly qualified and hold a degree in therapy. They know exactly what they are doing. On the other hand, in India, the young women who took the therapy sessions were probably no more than high school graduates. I doubt it very much if they knew the role the brain plays in a stroke. Often, I had to instruct them myself on how to correctly lift my limbs affected by the stroke.

Looking back, it is difficult for me to accurately assess the value of stimulation therapy. I believe that it helped my leg and foot muscles together with other things such as brisk walking and physical therapy.

Alongside my physical rehabilitation, I was also evaluated by a clinical psychologist at the Dodd Hall. This was a part of hospital protocol. It was to ensure that patients could return to their regular jobs or get a recommendation for disability benefits for life. The task of the clinical psychologist was to evaluate patients for any cognitive deficits from the stroke. This evaluation was based on the patient's ability to solve complex problems based on his or her level of education and also detect any signs of dementia or other memory-related problems.

Short-term problems are often seen in stroke patients with left-brain stroke, similar to the one I suffered. The psychologist's office was well-equipped with puzzles, memory cards, and trick questions. Most of the puzzles or other cards required that I mark the correct answer in a given time. But my problem was different! As a right-handed person, having my right side become weak from the stroke posed a challenge. I was not yet equipped with the skills to answer the questions using my left hand, even if it was just drawing a tick mark! As a result, my score wasn't particularly high for puzzles or memory cards. I realized this only when my clinical psychologist suggested that I could apply for permanent disability. This was not at all appealing to me and politely told my psychologist the same. Eventually, it was sorted out and I was able to return to teaching at the OSU in six months.

In short, treatment after a stroke involves looking for potential underlying causes that can cause a stroke. Hypertension, diabetes, obesity, or heart irregularities are common risk factors. In case a patient is clear of these, then therapy is initiated towards strengthening various muscle groups in the body. While physical therapy strengthens the skeletal muscles primarily to make the patient self-sufficient in locomotive activities, occupational therapy sessions are geared towards enabling the patient to return to normal life. Cognitive therapy is focused on improving various brain functions. All these three forms of therapy are very important and go a long way in ensuring that a stroke victim can return to normalcy as soon as possible.

What the hospital taught me as a stroke victim

While I was recovering at the OSU hospital, I participated in a weekly seminar for stroke victims. The sessions were conducted by experts who would visit the hospital and talk to the patients about the consequences of suffering from a stroke.

The talks ranged from what is a stroke and differences between ischemic and hemorrhagic strokes to discussions on early recognition of a stroke such as a sudden onset of facial weakness, inability to keep up one or both arms, abnormal speech patterns, headache, or seizures. They also discussed various risk factors such as high blood pressure, high cholesterol levels, diabetes, and atrial fibrillation.

I had none of these risk factors, yet I suffered a stroke. As I mentioned before, my stroke was the result of a congenital defect. So, when people ask me if I am still on medication, I have to inform them that there is no medication for the stroke per se. Medicines are given to patients to control risk factors or treat consequences of a stroke, such as in my case, an elevated heart rate. To combat this, I need to take a beta-blocker, a drug to normalize my heart rate. Here, I would like to share four important lessons that I learned while attending seminars at the hospital.

No two strokes are similar

A stroke depends upon several factors such as the way a blood clot occludes blood flow to the brain, the size of the clot, the region of the brain suffering suffocation, the amount of time involved in suffocation, the nature of rupture in the blood vessels rupture, and the time involved in oxygen deprivation to the brain cells. All these factors determine the type of stroke and its severity. It is because of these reasons that no two strokes should be compared.

There is an important lesson to be learned here. While someone might suffer a very mild stroke and recover within a few weeks, another with a severe stroke may never recover, or worse, die. So, comparing your condition with that of your neighbor who might have recovered in a few weeks is a fruitless exercise. It is only likely to cause you depression, rather than helping you in any way.

You can become abusive

A key quality required for dealing with a stroke victim is patience. Every person deals with the consequences of a stroke differently, and it is not uncommon for a stroke patient to become abusive, even with those who try to help him or her. There may be an outburst of raw emotions, the manifestation of frustration at not being able to use a limb, or simply an expression of anger for not being able to do things, one used to do earlier. I recall a young stroke victim at the therapy center shouting and cursing the people who were helping him and managing his wheelchair. It was simply his way of dealing with the consequences of the stroke. In such cases, therapy can help immensely along with love and patience from family and friends.

You may cry for no apparent reason

The therapists also told us that it is also not uncommon for a stroke victim to become over-emotional or cry over little things. Some patients will also break down easily for no apparent reason. In my case, it was timely and pertinent advice. I had become too emotional and would cry very easily. It would take as little as someone asking me how I was feeling or when the stroke happened or my plans for teaching again to make me cry.

An incident comes to mind. One cold February morning, I was at Martha More House for a therapy session. The outside temperature was -13 degrees Fahrenheit. I was barely fifteen minutes into therapy when the fire bells started to sound, and we had to evacuate the building and go outside. Since I was a wheelchair-bound patient, a therapist had to wheel me out. At the moment, something inside me snapped and I started sobbing. My therapist reassured me that it was probably because I couldn't bear the cold weather. But I was sinking into a whirlpool of self-pity. *How can I put myself in this situation? How did I become so helpless?* Naturally, there were no simple answers to my questions. It took a long time for me to realize that it was not me who put myself in that situation. I was not to blame for my condition. I think it took me about six years after the stroke before I could comfortably talk about it without being overwhelmed by emotions.

Rehabilitation

Assuming there are no underlying risk factors, the only recourse available to stroke victims is to relearn life's skills to go back to living life like before. This may or may not happen for every individual's journey with stroke is different. However, rehabilitation therapy helps patients comprehend and adapt to their new reality. A variety of experts in physiotherapy, occupational therapy, speech therapy, and orthopedics work together to help a patient deal with crises, big and small—dysfunctional or paralyzed limbs, inability to do mundane everyday tasks such as putting on clothes or shoes, and so on.

I cannot end this chapter without narrating an incident that happened during a stroke briefing-class in the hospital. On this particular day, my wife had dropped me off for the class and left. But even after fifteen minutes of waiting, the therapist did not show up. There were about ten to fifteen of us in the room—all wheelchair-bound. Everyone around me was calm but I felt a wave of panic rising inside. The thought of having to wait for forty-five minutes in the room was extremely distressing for me. It was probably because I felt completely helpless. I couldn't leave if I wanted to. Fortunately, the classroom door was open and I saw Dr. Sharon McDowell pass by. I shouted for her to rescue me. She rolled my wheelchair back to my hospital room. Later on, when I narrated this incident to a physiotherapist friend of mine, she taught me how to roll the wheelchair on my own. That way in case of an emergency, I would not have to rely on others to roll my wheelchair. It was not easy an easy skill to master because of my weak right hand, but I learned it nevertheless.

7

POST-STROKE MEDICAL PROCEDURES

My son Samir was in charge of taking all critical medical decisions in my living will at the time of my coma. As a doctor himself, I know he was the right person for the task. When he rushed to Ohio from California after learning about my stroke, one of the first decisions he had to make was regarding the type of feeding tube to be used on me. Since I was in a coma, there were two ways of ensuring that I get the nutrition my body needed. The first choice was to insert a nasogastric tube for feeding, but this had the disadvantage of inducing aspiration pneumonia. The second option was gastronomy, a surgical procedure in which a PEG tube is placed connecting the abdominal wall to the stomach. Though not risk-free as it carries a risk of an infection at the site where stomach tissue is sewn to the skin surface, my son preferred gastronomy for me. On his recommendation, a feeding tube was inserted into my abdomen through which semi-solid food of about 1,700 calories per day was given to me.

Doctors continued using the feeding tube, even when I was awake because stroke patients sometimes have swallowing complications. Many suffer from a disease called dysphagia which makes normal eating procedures such as chewing, tasting, and swallowing difficult. Before I was allowed to eat solid foods, doctors wanted to ensure that I was able to chew and swallow food the right way. For this, a short test was done, which I discussed in Chapter 6. But even after I started eating orally, my doctor advised against removing the feeding tube immediately. Since the hanging tube caused me no pain or discomfort as such, I did not mind it as much. The only inconvenience was at the time of bathing. Imagine taking a bath with a foot-long tube hanging out of your abdomen! It was after a few weeks of going home that my doctors finally permitted me to remove the feeding tube. The removal of the tube in the hospital was a bit of an anticlimax—if I can call it that.

On December 12, I had an appointment with a surgeon at the gastroenterology department. I expected the procedure to be long-drawn or at least involving some sort of surgery. At 6 am sharp, I reached the hospital. After completing the initial registration process, I went to the surgery room. A nurse helped me into a surgical gown and informed me that the doctor was on his way. When he finally reached after two hours, he briefly explained the process for the removal of the tube. There was no surgery involved! He would simply roll the hanging portion of the tube in his hands and then in one swift motion yank it out! The pain would be somewhat like being hit by a tennis ball on the stomach. "It's just a matter of ten seconds," he told me.

I closed my eyes and readied myself mentally. The doctor pulled. There was a booming sound and I felt an intense pain for a few seconds. Then it was ok. It was done and I was home by 10 am.

After reaching home, I took a look at my abdomen. Except for an indent, sort of like a navel, there was nothing else to show that up until a few hours back, there was a tube going into my stomach. Within a few days, the abdominal wall healed on its own. The depression in the abdominal wall is there even after twelve years, but the hole in the abdominal wall is, of course, sealed. On the whole, the tube-removal episode was rather amusing for me. It was over in a jiffy!

There is another interesting point I want to raise here. Since my stroke caused stiffness and rigidity in my right leg and hand, my doctors consulted with a specialist for Botox injections in my right leg. Contrary to popular perception, Botox is not just used in the beauty industry to reduce facial wrinkles. Studies have shown that Botox injections in the limbs and fingers can decrease muscle stiffness and rigidity found in stroke patients. Doctors believe that about thirty percent of stroke patients who suffer from muscle spasticity can be helped by this procedure. Even though the effects of Botox are temporary, they can be administered from time to time for muscle relief.

In my case too, it was decided that I would receive Botox injections at three weeks' intervals. The first instance was at the time of my stay at the Dodd Hall. I received two hundred units of Botox (botulism toxin A) in the gastrocnemius muscle in my right calf. However, I did not notice any improvement in my leg after the procedure. Even so, it was decided that I would be given three more Botox injections. Sadly, there wasn't any discussion on the subject and I was not informed of any additional cost for this procedure. So, it came to be as a surprise when I was billed $666 (my insurance paid the rest—a whopping amount of $6,801). Given the large sum involved, I believe that it should have been discussed with me, more so because I did not see any improvement in my right leg functions after the Botox treatment.

Over the years, I have found many strange practices in the healthcare business. It is the only business in which a client (patient) is asked to pay up *before* the course of treatment is decided! It is also the only business in which a patient has no idea at all about the amount he will be billed at the end of the treatment.

All this is very unfortunate because a patient may not be at his best in terms of his/her mental capacity. This is more so for patients of severe medical conditions like a stroke. There can be a lack of sharpness of the mind. Under such circumstances, it is easy to fall prey to scams or be billed unnecessarily for services of little use to the patient. This happened in my case too.

My earliest interaction with vendors was at the time discharge from Dodd Hall. The vendor provided me with a booster toilet seat and other gadgets for home use. In addition to this, there was also a brand new wheelchair. But I had not asked for any of these things. Neither did anyone discuss the cost of these utilities with me. For example, I paid $125 every month to the vendor for using the wheelchair—this was in addition to what he was charging my insurance company. It is outrageous because I could have simply bought a new wheelchair for as little as $99 during the Christmas promotion at Walgreen.

My run into another vendor was at Martha More House. My therapist had suggested that I use an electric stimulator at home. She informed me that a vendor would provide the stimulator and all I had to do was sign on a form. Even though she said that it would be taken care of by my insurance company, I used to receive monthly bills for its use until I returned it to the vendor. To make things worse, I don't think the equipment helped my muscles in any way.

Dealing with hospital vendors

The key thing to remember while dealing with any hospital vendors is to read the Terms and Conditions carefully. In my case, it seems there was a blank space on the form that I did not notice while signing the form. This blank space was used to fill in the monthly rental fee, which was not discussed with or disclosed to me. My advice is that if you don't have time to read all the Terms and Conditions or cannot comprehend them because of your ailment, it is better to not sign at all. If at all you must sign, be sure to cross out any blank spaces before signing on a document.

There was another procedure that I underwent in the months following my discharge from the hospital—a gamma knife surgery.

My stroke occurred due to the presence of an arterio-venous malformation (AVM) in my brain stem. An AVM occurs when arteries directly get connected to veins, bypassing the usual capillary system. In my case, the AVM caused bleeding in the brain, destroying brain neurons controlling the right side of my body. My doctors ruled out neurosurgery to stop the bleeding because the affected area in the brain stem was too close to neurons that controlled my respiration and vascular system. To potentiate the area, they suggested gamma knife surgery.

Gamma knife surgery treatment proliferates endothelial cells in the vasculature and reduces its size. It is also called radiosurgery, even though it is not an invasive procedure. It uses beams of gamma radiation to treat any lesions in the brain. Gamma knife surgery is not only a treatment for AVMs but is also used to treat brain cancers and tumors, trigeminal neuralgia (a disease in which nerve pressure causes intense facial pain), and noncancerous brain lesions.

A week before the actual gamma knife surgery, I had to sign a consent form that stated possible dangers of the surgery—bleeding, blindness, cessation of respiration, cardiovascular collapse, or death. For the first time in my life, I found myself frightened of a procedure. Nothing listed on the consensus form seemed to be a desirable outcome!

After three days of mulling over whether or not I wanted to go ahead with the surgery, I decided to take a leap of faith. I believed in God and the OSU. After all, if I could not trust the OSU—the institution where I taught for over four decades—where else could I go. I signed the consent form and my surgery date was fixed for the third week of February.

It was decided that my surgery would be carried out at the OSU cancer hospital in the presence of a radiation oncologist, my neurosurgeon, and a physicist. Though the surgery was only about forty-five-minutes' long, the preparation took almost thirteen hours. To undergo the procedure, my head was fitted with a heavy metal frame weighing about two pounds. I had to wear this for twelve hours that day.

Around mid-morning, I was wheeled into the brain angiogram room. For the angiogram, a catheter was inserted through a blood vessel in my thigh. For the next couple of hours, my doctors created a computerized mapping of my gamma knife surgery treatment.

After having lunch and relaxing for a few hours, the metal frame on my head was secured to a gamma knife bed. The gamma knife bed then slid into the Gamma Knife Perfexion machine, which was akin to a cylindrical tube used for taking MRIs. I was asked not to move my head. This is the reason for fitting the crown-like frame. With the frame, it is not possible to move and the gamma radiations can be focused onto the exact spot in the brain. Two hundred beams of gamma radiation from different angles were directed onto the AVM in my brain stem. Though I felt no discomfort or pain during the treatment, I was thinking about the fatalities written in the consent form and praying to God that it will all end well. The gamma radiation was given periodically for about forty-five minutes.

Since the effects of a gamma knife surgery take a couple of months to be apparent, my neurosurgeon scheduled another brain angiogram three months later. The second angiogram would tell me whether or not the surgery was successful in narrowing the openings of my AVM.

When I returned three months later for another brain angiogram, good news greeted me. The neurosurgeon was pleased and told me three things: first, the angiogram was perfectly executed; second, my risk of getting a second stroke was as much or as little as any normal human being (including my neurosurgeon himself); and third, there was no need to return to him (unless, of course, I wanted to drop by to say hello!).

These three sentences had a very positive impact on my psyche. I started believing in myself. Ever since that day, my recovery has seen an upward curve. This brings me to an important phenomenon.

Placebo is a little-understood phenomenon, even though it a common part of clinical trials. There's a reason why I want to talk about placebo here. Being a pharmacologist, I have always wondered, how a placebo pill produces a pharmacological effect. Is it merely the thought of going to a caregiver that helps a patient? Do patients perceive getting a real drug in a double-blind trial? Does the optimism of getting better with the drug treatment help the patient? There are many questions, but before I delve further, let's look at what placebo is.

A placebo is a dummy or sugar pill that looks like a real medical drug and comes in the form of a tablet or capsule. It has no active ingredients and is supposed to be pharmacologically inactive. Scientists who discover new drugs need to evaluate drug response and compare it to the response produced by a placebo, usually in a double-blind clinical trial, in which neither the patient nor the researcher knows who is getting a drug or placebo. The mystery is that on average 30 percent of patients get pharmacologically better on a placebo tablet, compared to the drug being evaluated.

For example, there is a concept known as placebo analgesia where placebo treatment is seen to reduce pain in patients. The treatment with a placebo is also effective in people suffering from depression. For people suffering from irritable bowel syndrome, the placebo response rate could be from anything from 16 percent to 71 percent. About 16 percent of patients with Parkinson's disease are said to feel better on placebo. Patients in clinical trials with antiepileptic drugs have a variable placebo response that has varied from zero to 19 percent.

To understand this further, a placebo effect has been seen to produce a physiological response; for example, a change in heart rate or blood pressure. Diseases that compel a patient to self-report an improvement, such as pain, anxiety, and depression (sometimes also associated with stroke) are markedly improved with a placebo.

A placebo effect generally depends on a patient's anticipation. If you are an optimistic person and anticipate positive results from the drug, you will feel better. On the other hand, someone who is a pessimistic person might end up worrying about the side-effects of the drug, and as a consequence, experience them. This is known to have happened in placebo clinical trials though the placebo directly does not cause these changes seen in the patients.

It is not uncommon to hear patients say that feel better simply by visiting a doctor's clinic, even if they have not taken any actual drug. Sometimes, we may feel that a doctor's words are very soothing. This is what precisely happened to me. After the gamma knife procedure to repair my AVM, I underwent a brain angiogram for the second time to check on the success of the surgery. When I heard my doctors say that he was pleased with the results, and my neurosurgeon told me that I was "normal," just like anyone else, I instantly felt like I had defeated the stroke. They were golden words to me. I was ecstatic and started having more confidence in my recovery than before.

Studies have shown that people with an optimistic view in life live a healthy life, have fewer health problems, and a lower rate of death. Optimistic people are also more responsible for their day to day life. They have more physical activity, don't smoke too much, drink alcohol in moderation, and eat a healthier diet. They can also cope with stress better than pessimistic fellow beings. However, not everyone is wired the same way. Not everyone is used to looking at the brighter side of life. Some people may perceive an episode as a glass-half-empty scenario while others see it as half-full. But I will only say this: train your mind to look for positivity. If you lack this attitude, then try to change your outlook and you will find those things to be grateful for—every day.

This reminds me of the laughter clubs started by Dr. Madan Kataria, a doctor from Mumbai, and the one who started the Laughter Yoga Clubs movement in

1995. This movement started with just five people but now has over sixty thousand different clubs all over the world. Many years back, I had visited a laughing club along with my friends in Nagpur, India. It was a wonderful experience. By positive thinking and laughter, my friends in this club were trying to improve their mood, boost their energy level, and improve their physical health. I found them to be resilient, creative, and take negative things lightly in life. They were also grateful to those who helped them out in life.

Doctors have reported that patients with an optimistic outlook in life can better cope with diseases, whether it is arthritis, or asthma, or fibromyalgia. On the other hand, pessimistic people have more of the stress hormone cortisol in their bodies. Some doctors have also reported a positive correlation between optimism and longevity. People with a positive attitude in life live longer. Optimism brings happiness and satisfaction, as well as a feeling of psychological well-being and good physical health. They may also lead to healthier lifestyles and stay away from substance abuse. I have always tried to embrace optimism in my life, and this has certainly helped me in my post-stroke recovery journey.

8

A LITTLE HELP ALONG THE WAY

In one swift stroke, my life changed in ways I could never have imagined. What I had taken for granted previously in my life suddenly became tasks I had to unlearn and relearn. Walking, eating solid food, writing—all these commonplace things were no longer mundane activities for me. They were stumbling blocks that reminded me every day of the ordeal I had suffered. After the initial disbelief of what had happened to me, I realized I could face my hurdles, even if with the help of some aids. These aids came to me in many forms—some tangible like my walking cane and leg brace, and others intangible, like the kindness of the social worker who advocated for my case at the OSU and ensured that I was allowed to stay at the hospital for five extra days till I was mentally ready to go home and urinate by myself, or the friendship I cultivated with a young couple in my city. I would like to talk about some of the aids that helped me overcome my constraints, and they might be useful to others in a similar situation.

During my initial days at the rehabilitation center, I was unable to stand on my own. The few steps I would walk were with the assistance of three individuals. Most of the time, I was confined to a wheelchair as the right side of my body had become very weak. This is a common aftermath of a stroke, and many victims have trouble with using one or the other side of their body, if at all. Being right-handed, this also meant that I was unable to write—a handicap that caused me a great deal of stress at the time.

My right hand had become limp, almost lifeless, and I could barely stretch the fingers of this hand. My fingers would curl up in a fistball. To remedy this, my doctor prescribed a brace for my right hand. It was a contraption that helped straighten my fingers. The brace on my arm used to come halfway in between my elbow on the arm and the wrist. I wore it on my hand, every night, for more than three years. My right hand is still weak and fingers still curl up, but whenever I realize this, I consciously stretch them out.

Specialists also advised daily exercises to strengthen my right hand, such as lifting my arm sideways and opening and closing the fist about twenty times a day. Twelve years down, it is still the first thing I do every morning when I wake up. Initially, I could not even touch any of the fingers of my right hand with the thumb. But now I can do this for the first three fingers. I have achieved this after immense hard work. I am also able to use my thumb and index finger to sign my name. This helped me tremendously in rebuilding my self-esteem as I can now use these two fingers to write checks and pay my monthly bills independently.

Looking back at those initial days at the hospital I realize I have come a long way. I remember I used to visit the common room of the hospital occasionally to access a desktop to check my email. It was a very frustrating exercise because I had no use for my right hand and no experience of using the left one. As a result, the cursor would fly all over the screen when I tried using my left hand. Equally challenging was using a pen. Having been a right-handed person all my life, I was now forced to use the other hand. It made me feel like a child learning to write for the first time!

It has taken me months of hard work to get accustomed to using my left hand for daily chores. In addition to strengthening my right hand, I also started practicing writing with my left hand. I started with the letters of the English alphabet. It took slow but consistent effort before I could write my name with my left hand. I also practiced using my left hand to access the computer.

Now, I also use both my right and left hands for eating, depending on what is on my plate! For moderately tough foods, especially those that require more maneuvering such as tearing pieces of an Indian flatbread, I prefer to use my left hand as I can use it with consistency and rhythm associated with eating and enjoying food. For cereals and milk, or boiled oat meals, I use right hand. But for other kinds of tough foods, or using a steak knife for meats, my wife usually helps me out.

The stroke also took away the coordination in my right and left foot. When I was brought to the Rehabilitation Centre, I was wheelchair-bound but by the time I went home, I was able to walk a few steps, even though with difficulty. I had what is known a foot drop—I had trouble lifting the front part of the right foot and would drag it on the ground when I walked. This meant I had to raise my thigh, as though climbing steps, to help the foot clear the floor. My doctor informed me that this unusual gait could lead to falls, and so I should wear an Ankle Foot Orthosis (AFO) foot brace.

I started using an AFO, which is a leg brace to support my ankle and foot, within two weeks of being discharged from the hospital. For this, I took an appointment at Hanger Inc., a clinic that designs

AFOs for the orthotic and prosthetic needs of stroke patients. I was recommended a rigid plastic AFO, which would provide support and ensure proper joint alignment of the foot and ankle. When I visited them, they took measurements of my entire leg (ankle and foot included) and used a Plaster of Paris-like substance to create a mold. It immediately solidified into a cast and was then used to make a plastic orthosis that would help support my weak leg. The orthosis was ready within a few weeks and came with two Velcro belts to fix it over my leg. I had to discard all my shoes with laces and buy new -Velcro ones—one-half larger in size and wider across. They also had attached Velcro to accommodate my new AFO. Thankfully, the AFO stabilized my foot. I am now on my third AFO and use it daily, even twelve years after the stroke.

After about three months of being mostly confined to a wheelchair, I decided to try walking with the help of a cane. It was a success! In fact, I still use a cane when I am outdoors. It is particularly useful when I have to climb up or down a staircase without a railing and in snowy conditions or on icy surfaces, not uncommon in Ohio in the winters. After the stroke, I cultivated a habit of walking for an hour in my neighborhood, and using a cane gives me more stability. It has made me more confident about walking on my own.

My foldable Hurrycane brand cane with its tripod base is a favorite of mine though little noisy. It gives me greater stability than the regular canes available elsewhere. These canes come to detachable rubber tips at the bottom that can be easily replaced with the help of a screwdriver.

Help came to me in many different ways. Some as I have mentioned here were tangible, such as my braces and walking canes. But there were others too—strangers who offered a helping hand when I needed it most.

There was an elderly lady at the hospital who used to come by to my room sometimes to enquire about me—how we were doing as a family and if we needed any help. I presumed she was a volunteer in the hospital. Later, I learned that she was a social worker appointed by the hospital to provide support and counseling for patients and their families if needed. She was there even to help with interpersonal relationships as well as educational and job-related problems.

My discharge from the hospital was scheduled in early November. However, even at this time, I was not able to urinate on my own. A nurse used to help me with a catheter and a kit to empty my bladder by gently pressing my abdomen. I was frightened by the thought of going home at a time when I could not even urinate on my own! So I requested my doctor to extend my stay in the hospital for five more days and conveyed the same to the hospital administrator through the social worker. She was very sympathetic to my cause and assured me that she would try to figure something out with the hospital staff.

Thankfully, I was granted the extension and allowed five days more at the hospital. Just two days before my scheduled discharge was I able to urinate at will. I was immensely relieved as it meant that I would not need a private nursing service at home. For this small personal victory, I owe thanks, not just to my doctor but also to my social worker. It was because of them that my medical insurance company agreed to extend my stay at the hospital.

Not just this, the social worker lady was also responsible for ensuring that my house was well-equipped to meet my new needs. She visited my home along with the physical therapy staff to advise on the required changes to the house. Since I was confined to a wheelchair, they wanted to make sure that my family had installed a proper ramp at the entrance of the house. The idea was to make me as independent as possible—I should be able to safely enter and exit on my own in case of an emergency. They also ensured that stair handrails were installed.

She also applied for a disability card for me at Central Ohio Transit Authority (COTA). Back then I had not understood the need for it. But in hindsight, my trips on the COTA bus were a blessing in disguise, not only for the convenience they offered but also for helping me realize that despite my shortcomings I had much to be grateful for. When I was finally discharged on

November 20, 2008, from the Rehabilitation Hospital, one of my friends gave me a ride home. But instead of going home, she drove me straight to the COTA office in downtown Columbus where I received my ADA identity card. Then I forgot all about it.

It was a few weeks later when I had to start therapy at Martha More House when I realized that my handicap meant I was entirely dependent on friends to drive me around. Since Sarla does not drive, I was usually ferried by one or another friend including Kishin Gursahaney. This went on for six months, until one day while at the therapy center, I noticed the COTA buses dropping and picking up disabled passengers. When I asked a fellow disabled person, he informed me that anyone with a disability could request the mini-COTA bus pick and drop them at a nominal fee. This was very good news!

When I finally started taking these buses, I was already off the wheelchair and I used a walking cane for support. It was not difficult for me to board or de-board these buses. But even for those using wheelchairs, these buses were completely secure. Not only would it pick up these passengers from their doorstep, once on the bus the driver would also secure the wheelchair to the floor of the bus with special equipment so that there was no chance of the wheelchair rolling back and forth in a moving bus.

In short, the COTA bus was a God-sent for me. It would pick me up from my driveway and drop me off at the hospital. I was no longer dependent on anyone else. The only drawback was the occasional waiting time. If the pick-up was scheduled at 9 am, it could very well reach at 8:30 am or at 9:15 am. But I did my best to utilize this time. Whenever I had to take a COTA bus, I would walk for thirty to sixty minutes on my porch or do some exercises with a pair of dumbbells.

I used the COTA bus service for two years before I could think about driving again. But for this, I had to relearn driving because, with my weak right side, it was not going to be possible to drive a regular unmodified car. Fortunately, the therapy department at Martha

More House offered a driver training program. My occupational therapist told me that I would now learn to drive using only my left leg and left hand to steer the car.

The first lesson I had was an evaluation of my map-reading and comprehension skills. I passed this test with ease, but the real challenge was yet to come! Before I could learn to drive again by using my left leg and arm, my therapists wanted me to drive a simulator car using an accelerator and steering wheel. This was no easy feat. Every time I hit the accelerator, my car would speed up and I would end up taking wide turns before crashing into one thing or another! It took a series of lessons on the simulator before I could drive safely at a low speed. This was followed by lessons from a therapist who specialized in teaching driving to stroke victims. I had a modified and specially equipped car to suit my special needs. The accelerator was on the right side of the brake so that I could use it with my left foot by pressing down on a rod connected to the right accelerator. The steering wheel was attached to a steering knob that facilitated steering with my left hand. On the right side of the car, there was an emergency brake that the therapist could use in case of an emergency. The therapist charged me a hefty $200 per hour that was not covered by insurance. He also offered me to come and help me for taking a driver's examination by the Ohio Bureau of Motor Vehicles for additional money. He figured out that I needed at least ten lessons. He would take me to empty parking lots of OSU buildings on the West campus where there were many empty spots for me to practice driving and maneuvering.

When I first learned driving in the United States, I learned driving as well as parallel parking. It seems they have abandoned teaching parallel parking in favor of maneuvering. I found maneuvering the car quite difficult. After about ten practice sessions, my therapy teacher took me to the BMV office for the road and maneuvering tests. I passed the road test but flunked the maneuvering test as my car had hit a traffic cone during the maneuvering test. I had to practice again a couple of times and retake the test which I passed. I was then eligible for a new driver's license.

My new license came with few restrictions that I cannot drive a vehicle that is not equipped with the accelerator on the right side of the brake for my left leg, and the car has to be equipped with a steering knob.

I had to take my old car to Columbus Mobility shop in Worthington to get it equipped with a left side accelerator for my left foot. They also installed a resting upside platform for my right foot to rest on the original accelerator, without pressing it, and a steering knob on the car to steer it with my left hand only. I started driving on my own sparingly as I was not comfortable with it in the beginning. I had no problem with familiar destinations, but driving to new destinations gave me butterflies in my stomach. It was difficult to follow GPS directions and drive. I was also apprehensive of crowded parking lots, parking ramps, and had trouble parking the car in my home garage.

In March 2013, I bought a new car and got all the new mobility gazettes (left side accelerator and a steering wheel knob) installed. The installation of these gazettes cost me about $550, which was reimbursed to me by the Honda Company because I bought a new car from them and applied for the reimbursement. After I bought the new car and practiced my driving—usually to run errands such as buying groceries or for going to the OSU for my job—I started feeling more confident in my driving ability. Gradually my anxiety on exceeding a speed of 40 miles per hour vanished. Now I have no problem driving but I don't drive more than 30 miles or 45 minutes at a stretch. In the last seven years, my car has put only about 26,000 miles. I have also acquired a disability decal and license plate showing disability, and park my car in the parking spots reserved for disabled people.

But not all helping hands came from therapy hospitals or specialists or professionals. Some just appeared in my life almost magically reaffirming my faith in humanity and the goodness of people. It had been about two weeks that I had returned home after spending about six weeks at the OSU hospital. One fine day, a young girl, Ekta Sharma, probably in her mid-twenties, called us on our landline and expressed a desire to visit us. Naturally, I was surprised. When I asked her this, she replied, "Everyone at Columbus is talking about Gopi Tejwani's stroke. My husband and I stay nearby and we really want to meet you!"

When she visited, she told us that she was a nursing student and her husband worked in the software industry. She had heard about my predicament and wanted to help out, whether it be with movement, exercise, therapy, driving, or any other kind of help I needed! I was pleased to hear this and readily accepted her help. Very soon, she started helping me with my exercise and therapy regimen.

To cut a long story short, the young couple has been helping us for the last twelve years. She and her husband Manoj Jagwani, are like our adopted children and help us whenever we need them. From opening a can to driving me to a hospital for my appointment—they have done it all. Thanks to them, my wife and I have met other young couples who address us as "uncle" and "aunty" and are always willing to extend their help in whatever way possible.

They have now two children of their own. The kids are a joy to be around! They visit us often and light up our lives with their presence. Their eldest child is barely four years old, and he already kneels and touches my feet and my wife's feet in customary Indian tradition to pay his respects. Understand that if you want to teach your child something—whether it is etiquette, generosity, or simply paying respects to elders—start very early in life. Before the Coronavirus outbreak, we would often go out to eat together or visit friends together. Every day I realize what a blessing it is to have the company of young people. Not only are they vibrant, energetic, and optimistic, they are also our harbingers for new technology! We now have many new young friends through this couple. They have been a blessing for us in more ways than one and have reinforced our belief in the goodness of strangers.

I sometimes wonder, what makes people do a random act of kindness? The answer may be in their upbringing and the way they were brought up as children. Though I am twice as older than the young couple in age, I have learned a great deal from them. The world will be far better if only there were more people like them.

9

THOSE NASTY FALLS

The type of stroke and the area of the brain affected play a vital role in the survival chances of a patient. Hemorrhagic stroke, in general, is more destructive than the ischemic stroke. I had a hemorrhagic stroke in the brain stem area—a twofold blow, because the brain stem is responsible for numerous vital bodily functions such as breathing, heart rate, blood pressure, speech, swallowing, hearing, and eye coordination. Thus, having a hemorrhagic stroke in this area could be fatal. Not only this, but the brain stem is also located next to the cerebellum, which is Latin for "little brain". It is a very important structure of the hindbrain responsible for coordinating voluntary movements, in addition to posture, balance, and other vital functions such as respiration, heart function, and blood circulation. Bleeding due to a hemorrhagic stroke in the brain stem area can also block oxygen supply to the neurons surrounding the cerebellum.

Balance is our ability to hold the body up and maintain proper posture at all times.

If we can maintain balance, we don't fall. Our brain is constantly relaying signals for the coordination of various muscle groups to maintain balance. A stroke hampers the ability of the brain to do this and stroke victims have a difficult time coordinating muscles and maintaining proper position and balance.

Soon after being discharged from the hospital, my physical therapy was focused on reclaiming my strength in the leg muscles. For this, my therapist made me do numerous activities and exercises. All these, my balance and posture. For example, he would drop a coin or a pen on the floor and ask me to pick it up. I also used an exercise bike to strengthen my leg muscles. Since my right arm and right leg had become very weak, he taught me how to get up from the floor in case of a fall. Ideally, I would take the support of a sofa or bed or some sturdy object to prop up myself. In case no such object was available, I could use the left palm to lift my body from the ground.

However, despite my vigorous physical therapy and balance exercises, I have had over fifty falls in the last twelve years. Some of them, even after being cautious, though a few falls could have been avoided, had I been more careful or been able to be careful. Luckily none of the falls caused any head injury or fractures.

One of my earliest falls was in my office at the OSU. Before my stroke, I was in the habit of taking books from the upper racks of a bookshelf by standing on a revolving chair. When I tried this after recovering from the stroke, I fell. My balance just wasn't good enough. With my weak right hand, I was unable to bring down heavy books from the bookshelf—it was the last straw that broke the camel's back as far as my retirement from the OSU was concerned. Even though I had no problems in teaching or my research, I knew it was time for me to retire when I realized that I could no longer carry heavy books or type using both hands.

For many stroke patients, bathrooms are hotbeds for potentially dangerous falls. I was no different. One of my most serious falls happened in my bathroom at home. It was soon after my discharge from the hospital, and naturally, I was very weak at the time. One morning while sitting on the toilet seat, I realized that I had not kept toilet paper within easy reach of my left hand. The toilet roll was on my right. What could I do? In an attempt to take the roll with my left hand, I twisted my body to the right and as a result, lost my balance. I could not grab the toilet seat in time and fell with a loud thud on the hardwood floor. Thankfully, my wife was in the adjoining room and she rushed inside and helped me up. From that day onward, I always ensured that there was enough toilet paper on my left side!

Another bathroom incident comes to mind. One of the many problems I face is using high bathtubs. If I am at a friend's place or in a hotel, I used to take help from my wife to get into the bathtub to take a shower. In 2014, my wife and I were visiting friends in Florida. It was early in the morning and my wife was still asleep. I wanted to take a shower so decided to use the bathroom wall as support to get into the bathtub. So far so good. It was only when I was done and was climbing out of the tub that bad luck struck me. My hands were wet from the shower and when I used it to support myself against the wall, it slipped on a glossy tiled wall and I fell with my head hitting the toilet seat. Thankfully, the toilet seat was padded so I got off with just a bump on the head! But nothing compares to my bathroom fall while traveling in India. Most Indian houses have wet bathrooms with marbled flooring that can be very slippery. I experienced this firsthand when I slipped over a small piece of soap and fell to the ground biting my tongue in the process!

Ironically one of my more serious falls happened while in therapy. It was a physical therapy class and I was given the task to walk briskly. My instructor used to hold me up with a waist belt during the exercise. On that fateful day, the walk was a little too brisk and a bit too long. My foot drop in the right leg caused me to fall, and unfortunately, my instructor was not able to break my fall. I fell hard. I had a bleeding bruise on my nose and forehead, which took almost ten days to heal.

However, none of these falls were as bad as the one I had while visiting Nagpur, India, where I was hit by a car because of my inability to move away as quickly as the driver would have liked me to! In another instance, I hurt myself when I fell onto a hard concrete floor while climbing out of the backseat of a two-wheeler scooter.

Living here, one does not realize that the United States is a haven for disabled people. I have traveled to over sixty countries in my life, but never have I seen a country more humane than this in its treatment of disabled people. In fact, in many countries, people barely have any patience to show courtesy to disabled people.

The frequency of my falls has decreased from one fall per month to a fall once or twice a year. Over the years, I have learned to be very careful and not do things in a rush. I am very cautious while climbing up or down staircases, and always hold the railings when I do. I also allow myself a couple of minutes before I get out of bed in the morning. This helps me balance better and be more aware of my surroundings, especially in a new place. The body changes after a stroke so it is pointless to be upset over things I could do in the past, but no longer can. For example, I can't lift heavy objects and climb up a staircase, so I don't even try. It is better to be careful than to be sorry! I also continue to wear my leg braces for support and use my cane, especially when going for long walks, walking on uneven surfaces, or taking stairs without railings.

My wife is also a senior citizen now. It's been a decade since she first told me that she is finding it difficult to negotiate the stairs in our multi-story home. Besides, after the stroke, I wasn't too sure about my ability to take stairs. With all this in mind, we decided to shift to a new ranch type of home. We built a new house in Dublin, a city near Columbus Ohio. We decided to move in April 2020. Unfortunately, with the ongoing pandemic, it was a hassle. On the day of moving to the new house, the movers had kept our belongings on the driveway to the house. I happened to notice a large plastic bag that I wanted to put in a trashcan nearby. It was a windy day and just when I was about to throw the bag, it flew from my hand. As I tried to grab it, I lost my balance and fell backward. The area was strewn with gravel and small stones. I fell left-hand first on the ground. There were cuts on the fingers and some of the skin from my middle finger had come off.

This incident forced me to introspect. Why did I fall? I learned three lessons from this accident. First, it is *not* worth chasing an empty plastic bag. Second, I cannot be an impulsive person at my age and with my condition. Third, I should be mindful of my surrounding surface areas.

I have been mindful of all these things ever since, but despite that, I had another fall on 29 May 2020. After the stroke in 2008, I have cultivated a habit of walking in my neighborhood for an hour daily. The neighborhood where my previous house was located was fully developed with sidewalks. I never had any trouble walking there; however, the new one is still developing with many houses being constructed presently. The sidewalks are also yet to be developed. The roads are full of dirt and heavy construction equipment. Sometimes, they block the road with big equipment, and in such cases, one has to either go around the equipment or leave the road and walk over uneven surfaces.

One day the dirt road I was walking on was blocked with a piece of heavy equipment. I realized that to walk down further, I could either go through an opening about four to five feet high or take the uneven surface along the road. The latter looked risky so I decided to go through the opening by bending a little. Sadly, it turned out to be the wrong decision. Just as I was bending my knees to go through the opening of the Savco soil digger, my knees gave under and I collapsed on the dirt road, landing on my left hand and left knee. There was not too much bleeding from my hand, and only some bruises on the left knee all thanks to the long pants I was wearing that day. But I was in a state of shock for ten minutes. There wasn't a soul in the vicinity, and I could not get up on my own without a solid three-foot-high support. The only way was to crawl on the dirt road back to the soil digger so that I could take its support and get up. I learned an important lesson that day: for a stroke victim, there can be a disconnect between the mind and the body. You may think it is doable because it was easy in the past or maybe it doesn't look very challenging, but that might not be the case.

This was a bitter pill to swallow because, throughout my life, I have been an adventurer and a risk-taker. I have jumped into a water-well without being much of a swimmer, jumped off a moving truck without realizing that I should jump in the direction of the truck and not against it, climbed tall trees without knowing that it is easier to climb than coming down! After a certain age, the body simply does not cooperate with the active mind. It reminds me of my octogenarian friend who fell on a hard floor simply because she presumed that she could tie her laces standing up! For most of us, the body deteriorates physically first before our mind. One has to realize that merely presuming that you can accomplish a task is not good enough. The body may not cooperate because it may be much out of shape or too old or simply out of the practice. Before beginning any task, take a minute to consider the consequences. Don't be impulsive. Saving a minute or two minutes is counter-productive at times because you may end up spending more time and enduring pain.

Just as a child must learn to do things on his own, a stroke victim may also have to relearn many things, including basic bodily functions as well as activities such as walking, eating, speaking, and many other things. Therapists have an important role to play because they provide physical, occupational, cognitive, and speech therapy, but even so, they have their limitations. A therapist cannot be with his patients 24/7. This task usually falls on the partner, as it was in my case. After I had my stroke, it was my wife who was with me at all times.

I went into a coma immediately after my stroke. At that time, I was dependent on medical and nursing support for everything, including eating, defecation, urination, and cleaning. It was only after I regained consciousness that the real challenges started. I had to re-learn everything from scratch.

Fortunately for me, swallowing was not a problem. Once my doctor gave me a go-ahead for eating solid food, I was no longer dependent on the food tube inserted in my abdomen. Having said that, I still had to adapt to my new reality of a partially paralyzed and weak right side. For a right-handed person, to suddenly switch to my left hand was challenging. To make up for the loss of use of my right side, I had to modify my behavior in some ways. To give you an example, let me demonstrate how I make my morning tea. I like my tea with milk. But for this, I need to open the refrigerator. If I open it using my left hand, how do I take out the milk bottle? We have a one-gallon milk bottle, which weighs almost four kilos or nine pounds—I can't lift that much weight with my right hand. Neither do I possess the grip or strength to open the refrigerator door with this hand.

So, what can I do?

I have two options. Open the refrigerator with my left hand. Keep it open and then bring out the milk bottle with the same hand. Return to the table and pour milk into my teacup, then take it back and close the door. The second option is to train the right hand to open the door and take out the milk with the left hand. I have tried this but for me, it is not easy to train the right hand as it is easy to train the left. With constant practice, however, I find that my right hand is getting better in opening a refrigerator now. I make my breakfast every day.

I had to also train myself to eat with my left hand. I use my right hand only while eating simple foods such as cereals, oatmeal, or other very soft items. The main advantage of using my left hand is that I am able to maintain a steady rhythm that one enjoys while eating. The same thing is true for drinking fluids—I always use the left hand. With the right, there is always a fear of spilling, which can be dangerous with hot drinks.

I make my tea in the microwave oven. Initially, a hot cup of tea was difficult to carry, even for the left hand, because of my balance issues. I had to practice carrying a half a cup of the hot liquid for months. Then I graded it up to three-fourth for a couple of years. Nowadays, I can carry almost a full cup of hot fluids with my left hand if I am extremely careful. Carrying a filled cup with my right hand is still impossible.

Another challenge is my knife skills. As of now, I am unable to use either my hands to cut hard food items, like steaks, apples, and other hard fruits. I try to do this with my left hand but it is not easy at all. This is unfortunate because I love to cook. If I cannot chop fruits, vegetables, and meats, lift heavily loaded pans or open cans, then how can I cook? While I have not found all the answers, I have managed to find a circumvent many of my problems. For example, I use a battery-operated can opener to open cans.

This gadget is very useful as it is lightweight and very effective.

There is no drastic change in my dietary habits due to the stroke, except for an increase in high fiber foods and reduced alcohol intake. I never drink more than one drink per sitting per day. Usually, I restrict my alcohol intake to twice a week. Since I am already prone to tripping and falling (even when in control), I would rather not increase my chances by being inebriated! Also because I have started driving again, I like to be very cautious. I do not want to lose this privilege in life.

The stroke also had a tremendous effect on my smooth muscles in the gastrointestinal tract, which has made me prone to constipation. For this, I eat foods rich in fibers such as fruits, vegetables, and whole grains almost every day. I developed several high-fiber breakfast recipes that are listed in Chapter 11.

The most unfortunate part of the stroke was the realization that I cannot walk, write, drive, or use a computer. I felt as if my life was over. I thought I was confined to a wheelchair forever. When I went for physiotherapy for the first time, I had no balance or strength in my leg muscles and three therapists had to hold me up. But I certainly did not give up on hope. I continued my physiotherapy with the help of the therapist and exercise machines until I got sufficient strength in my leg. Even after returning home, I continued to go for walks in my neighborhood. Initially, it was for about thirty minutes a day. Gradually, I scaled it up to forty-five and now I walk for an hour every day. I have been doing this for the last twelve years. In fact, the days I cannot go for a walk, I feel miserable. I like walking around the campus and in the neighborhood, but in case the weather is very bad and I can't step out, I just walk inside the house, going from one room to the other, circling like a cat!

Just like the muscles of my leg, my right hand also suffered. Not only did this affect my ability to handle food or cook, but it also impacted my writing. I couldn't even sign my name using the right hand! So, I had to learn to write with my left hand for the first time in my life. After I returned home from the hospital, I started practicing writing with my left hand. Initially, it was just like a child's scribble. I would write 1,2,3, … 100 or a, b, c, … x, y, z. At least I wanted to be able to write checks and be able to pay my bills on my own. Within a few years, my thumb and index finger of the right hand gained sufficient strength—enough for me to write using these two fingers. Fortunately, computers and emails have obliterated the need for writing long letters or reports. This is a great boon for disabled persons like me.

The first time I used the computer after my stroke, was at the hospital during one of my occupational therapy sessions. When I tried using the mouse with my right hand, the cursor went berserk. I was trying to open one website but ended up opening a bunch of useless websites. I tried many times before realizing that it was a fruitless exercise. Thereafter, I started training my left hand to use the computer. In the beginning, it was difficult. But gradually, I learned how to use the left- and right-click buttons on the mouse and also typing words on the keyboard. Twelve years down the line, I continue to use my left hand and my index finger to type.

A key aspect of my post-stroke life is learning self-care. Because of my semi-paralyzed body, I could no longer do the things I could do in the past. For any stroke patient with partial paralysis, basic self-care activities such as bathing can become challenging. During my initial days in the hospital, I was given sponge baths by the nursing staff. Later on, I was able to take a weekly bath in the hospital with the help of my wife. Even after returning home, she used to help me bathe as I could neither apply soap on my body nor wipe myself dry with the towel. Slowly, I started using soap to clean the left side of my body with my right hand. Now, I can shower independently as long as it is a step-in type shower. But I have difficulty using bathtubs. If there is a grab-bar I can hold on to I use it to balance myself while standing on my weak leg, otherwise I need someone to help me in and out of the tub.

Eating, drinking, walking, sleeping, and driving independently gives me immense pleasure. When I was confined to a wheelchair, my biggest worry was whether or not I could ever drive again. Fortunately, I can do this now using my modified vehicle. I avoid driving to unknown places or driving in inclement weather, but other than this I have no trouble with my car. Even at night, I can drive safely and confidently.

Even though I am not as physically active as I used to be, I have not given up on my daily walks. I sleep better when I am physically tired. For this I must walk for at least one hour daily, rain or sunshine. The days I go to the mall (in addition to my walk), I get a very good night's sleep of six to seven hours at a stretch. The stroke affected the sleep center in my brain. It was apparent at the very early stages of the stroke when I was in the hospital. I would often wake up in the middle of the night and keep tossing and turning unable to go back to sleep. Even now, I have trouble sleeping at night. For anything more than four hours of sleep, I need to trick my body into a slumber! My walks certainly help. It also helps to have a clear, stress-free mind, do deep breathing exercises, and chanting.

To live a life of fulfillment, one needs to have a purpose. For me, my work at the OSU has always been a source of immense pleasure. As a professor at the OSU, I often wondered why anyone would retire! But after the stroke, I was drained both physically and emotionally to think about work. As a professor, my work involved writing/typing research grants and required a level of physical agility and strength. But I couldn't even lift big books, let alone read them. Earlier I could stand in the classroom and deliver a flawless lecture, but now that wasn't the case. After recovering, I forced myself to continue for four years, but there was little joy in it. My body was simply not able to take the strain of working long hours. At the time, I could not drive to campus and had to rely on the COTA Mainstream bus. This meant more time spent in commuting. So after thirty-two years of teaching and research, I decided to retire from a very active and fruitful academic life.

Teaching at the OSU was the only job I ever held and it gave me a great sense of purpose in life. So when the university offered me an emeritus faculty position, I readily accepted it. I still teach a short course to students on drug abuse once a week in the autumn semester. I still have a "hotel office", which is a common office for all emeritus professors who want to continue teaching. The university pays me a small honorarium for teaching, but more than that if through my course, I can discourage even a single student from taking drugs, it is worthwhile. I have now been at the OSU for more than forty-four years and enjoyed every moment of it.

For all my blessings, I am thankful to God. Most of my life I have done the research to prove or disprove my experimental hypothesis. On the God question, I cannot do this. I cannot prove the existence of God one way or another. But all I know is that I have faith in God, and it is this faith that helped me sail the rough seas in life. This, of course, does not mean that I sit around twiddling my thumbs leaving everything to the mercy of God. I have realized that God helps those who help themselves. As a stroke victim, the words "give up" should not be a part of your vocabulary. I can say from personal experience that improvements come in tiny increments but even if it's 0.01 percent progress daily, it is better than nothing at all. One has to be patient and keep trying. In the beginning, I could not touch the thumb of my right hand with the other fingers of the same hand. I could not write or lift any weight. But with lots of hard work, I can touch the thumb with the tips of my other fingers in the right hand, write again, and easily lift about ten pounds of weight. This might seem insignificant to an average person, but as someone who could not even pick up a toilet roll, I have come a long way. The mind plays a very important part in the recovery process of a stroke victim. Having a positive mindset is half the battle won. I have always tried to keep my optimism alive, even when everything seemed bleak. And I can say with certainty that this attitude has helped me.

One more thing, I have learned in life is the realization that there are people in the world who are not as fortunate as you. I can grumble on that my right leg and hand are weak or I cannot run or walk fast, but then I remember the two young blind girls on the COTA bus. I am grateful that I have my sight intact and can see and admire things around me. The stroke made me emotional and I can easily cry thinking about the sad events in life but I know I am getting stronger emotionally and physically and want to continue doing my bit to make the world a better place.

10

TRAVELING THE WORLD AFTER A STROKE

Had it not been for my untimely stroke, I would have visited South Africa in 2008 with Sarla and my friends. That never happened, and for some time, travel was the last thing on my mind. At the time, I was naturally reluctant to travel. The misfortune of my stroke was real and one I could not ignore, but time (and hard work) is a great healer so two years later, opportunity knocked on my door again.

Therapy and medication had helped me regain much of my strength and in early 2010; I knew I was ready to travel again. Of course, I had a new normal now. There were certain restrictions because the right side of my body was weak. For example, it was difficult for me to get up from the ground without the support of a sofa or a chair or another human being. There was also the fear of falling and hurting myself. So I knew I had to be extra cautious, such as always using a cane while walking.

International travel came with a set of unique challenges. However, I knew I had to brave them and make the best of what I had. Over the last decade, I have traveled to many countries, including multiple trips to my birth country, India.

My first vacation after the stroke was to Las Vegas and Mexico. It was two years since my stroke and my friends and I decided that I was ready to travel again. In January 2010, I mustered enough courage and joined a few friends to travel to Los Vegas and Mexico for ten days. It was a wonderful trip and everything went as per plan. In Las Vegas, I had no problems except walking along the Las Vegas Strip. I could not walk very fast, but I could walk for an hour or so without any problem. In Mexico, when we visited Cabos San Lucas in the Baja California area, my friends wanted to go parasailing. I could not attempt this because my right arm was too weak to hold on the parachute and my wife and friends too were apprehensive about it. I confess that I wanted to go, but I decided to heed the advice of friends and fellow travelers. Instead, I switched from the cruise to a small boat to go to the middle of the Pacific Ocean. The rest of the trip was wonderful and I especially enjoyed my visit to Puerto Vallarta and Cabos San Lucas in Mexico.

This trip's success encouraged me to attend a wedding in India in October 2010. Traveling in India came with a different set of challenges. To begin with, most people don't know how to deal with disabled people. Some might want to help out but are reluctant to express themselves. Others can be insensitive. I recall my ordeal while crossing a road in Pune city—not one vehicle stopped or gave me sufficient space to cross the street. Everyone seemed to be in a hurry or appeared lost in their thoughts.

I had an especially bitter experience in my hometown in Nagpur city. I was walking on a narrow street with the help of my cane when a car driven by a lady started honking. When I was unable to move fast enough for her, she simply drove past without caring that her side-view mirror hit me and my cane went flying up! Fortunately, she stopped the car. When I questioned her why she hit me, her response was outrageous. "I did honk and you did not move!" This lady equated honking to applying a break, and she failed to see that I could not move fast enough because there was a pile of sand lying on the road on my side!

In Bangalore, I took a fall because the curb of the sidewalk was too high for my right foot. Fortunately, a security guard posted there was kind enough to help me up.

Access to disability-friendly toilets and bathroom is another problem I faced in India. A harrowing experience was my overnight train journey from Nagpur to Agra in India. The train lacked Western-style toilets and it was impossible for me to use the squatting-style toilet because of my knee-length AFO. Luckily for me, I was with relatives and they helped me survive the train journey. I also had a nasty fall in a bathroom while in India. Most Indian households have wet bathrooms with marble or concrete floors. I was taking a shower when I slipped. The soap had made the floor very slippery. I fell as if in slow motion but had no way to break my fall. When I hit the ground, I bit my tongue and blood came spurting out of my mouth. Luckily, the tongue is a self-healing organ, and after a few days, it had healed on its own.

In 2010, I spent two months in India. My brother is a trustee in a local hospital in Nagpur, and he arranged massage therapy sessions for me. The masseur was an expert in his field and gave me a strong massage for about forty-five minutes daily for nearly two months. The massage therapy was strong enough that my body got tired, and it induced sleep in the middle of the day for me.

In fact, this was not my first experience with leg massage. During my early days at the Rehabilitation Hospital, a friend Ravinder and her husband, Balvinder, used to visit often. Ravinder is my former postdoctoral fellow who worked under me for five years at the

OSU. She and her husband were both visibly upset on learning about my stroke. During one of their visits, Balvinder, who is always smartly dressed in a necktie and all, simply rolled up his sleeves, soaked his hands with massage oil, and started to massage my weak leg. Each time they visited, Balvinder would massage my leg. This massage therapy continued for six weeks until I was released from the hospital. Though it is difficult for me to evaluate the long-term benefits of massage therapy on my body, I do feel that my right leg is much stronger and my balance has improved a great deal since my stroke twelve years back.

I also took the services of another therapist in Nagpur. The charge was only a dollar per session compared to the hundreds of dollars in the United States. I readily agreed thinking it would be beneficial to exercise in the presence of a qualified therapist and her associates. Though there was a marked difference in the quality of sessions in the United States and India, the staff was extremely helpful and assisted me as best as they could.

Another incident from one of my trips to India comes to mind. The AFO I was using was about two years old when I was in Nagpur. So my therapist suggested a local facility in Nagpur that made AFOs. The cost would be on a fraction of what I had paid for the original—a total of only $60 in place of the whopping $975 I paid in the United States (plus the charge incurred by my medical insurance company). I thought this a good deal and agreed to get one made. After several weeks when the AFO was ready to be picked up, I found it to be quite an inferior product made with cheap quality plastic as compared to the AFO made abroad. Not only this, the plastic bottom of my AFO was larger than needed. Whereas the American AFO increased my shoe size from 8.5 to 9, the Indian AFO increased it to 13! This also meant I had to buy larger shoes to accommodate the new AFO, which was quite uncomfortable. However, I didn't have to use it for long as it broke after a few months' use. The phrase "You get what you pay for" is cliché for good reason.

In India, there is one thing you will get for free. And, that is unsolicited advice. I was at a movie theatre in Pune. This was two years after my stroke—I had a limp and used a cane to walk. Moreover, my right arm was hanging sort of lifeless by my side. A man walked up to me and told me that if I should bathe my right arm with pigeon blood to cure myself of my handicap. I realize that such people probably mean well but are misinformed. I simply thanked him and moved on. I heard this 'pigeon blood' pseudoscience once again in Nagpur.

Another popular "cure" was visiting holy men. Not just strangers, I was even given this piece of advice by a relative who repeatedly insisted that I should pay a visit to one such holy man who had treated his father-in-law! The relentlessness took me by surprise, and it was only when I firmly refused to indulge him further that he backed off. But it made me wonder, how people who cannot even differentiate the liver from the brain, give such a drastic, unsolicited, and persistent advice. I once made the mistake of sharing my phone number with a stranger who wanted to help out. He claimed he knew a holy man who could cure my partially paralyzed body. Within two hours, I received the call from the *babaji* (holy man) saying that he was willing and eager to treat me. He even offered to come home and meet me. I had to politely decline his offer.

All this made me wonder about the mystery of treating a stroke. Medical science accepts that there is no treatment of a stroke. Instead, the treatment is for the underlying causes such as high blood pressure, diabetes, or drug abuse, which might have led to the stroke, and its after-effects, such as paralysis of limbs. The actual stroke may occur due to a clot blocking a blood vessel or rupturing of a blood vessel in the brain, but once the stroke has occurred, there is no treatment except to take care of the damage induced it. Depending upon the damage, it may take years of treatment, unlike many other diseases that can be treated in relatively shorter periods. So, I can see the frustration among people who are looking for alternative treatments.

The first thing they taught me when I was in the rehabilitation center that no two strokes are alike. A rule of thumb is to never compare one stroke with another. The second thing I learned was that while one stroke victim might recover in a few days or months, another might take years. So in that sense, stroke victims may heal from the damage caused by a stroke on their own, and taking bath with pigeon blood or invoking divine intervention maybe just a coincidence. Unfortunately, even educated people believe in such pseudoscience. From my experience, I can firmly say that it takes years of therapy, exercise, and hard work to reverse the damage caused by the stroke. There is no magic potion that will work.

With the acceptance that the stroke was my reality and I if I wanted to travel, I needed to make some adjustments or be willing to endure some discomforts, I was successful in traveling to many countries across America, Europe, Asia. In 2013, we visited Alaska and Canada. Most of our journey was by air, bus, or cruise and I had no trouble because of my disability. The only compromise I had to make was at Stanley Park in

Vancouver, where there was a wooden structure with long staircases going downhill. I had to skip visiting this side of the park as I was reluctant to negotiate so many stairs. In Italy too, I faced no problems except when taking water taxis or gondolas in Venice. But, even here, there were people who assisted me in my safe transfer to the boat.

In 2014, we traveled to a number of Hawaiian Islands and the city of Ensenada in Mexico. The same year, we took a memorable trip to the Canadian Rockies. We visited Lake Wharton, Banff, Jasper, and many more sites. Sadly, I had to forego the walk around Lake Peyote because of the rough terrain of the surrounding areas. My guide requested me to stay back on the bus. I also had a hard time walking over the Athabasca Glacier at the Columbia Icefield near Jasper. I did not have the correct shoes to do this and needed three people to hold me up. A minute into landing on the glacier, I abandoned the idea of walking on it and returned to the bus, so that the others could enjoy their time walking on the glacier.

The following year, we visited the beautiful country of Turkey. Though I had a tough time in some places, it was worth the trouble. One such experience was the hot air balloon ride in Cappadocia, which is famous for its natural earth formations. It was difficult for me to climb into the balloon basket and was lifted and "dumped" inside. Having said that, the gorgeous view from the top made up for all inconveniences. Pamukkale, famous for its "Cotton Castles," is a UNESCO World Heritage Site. The terraced thermal pools made from natural mineral deposits are certainly worth a visit. Though it was too slippery for me to step on, I did submerge my feet in the spring water for a few minutes.

I did not restrict my travels to the Western hemisphere. In 2016, we embarked on a trip to Thailand, Myanmar, Laos, and Cambodia. I had no problem visiting crowded places in Bangkok, even the Sleeping Buddha statue area. Myanmar too was trouble-free and I was able to comfortably walk without any problem. It was the same in Laos. I faced some difficulties while visiting the grand Angkor Wat temple complex in Siem Reap,

Cambodia. Many of the ruins had uneven ground and involved climbing over large boulders. I had to skip visiting some of the temples for this reason, especially the ones that involved climbing high staircases without a handrail. At Tonle Sap, which is a floating city near Siem Reap, it was hard for me to sit on the bullock cart—the choice of transportation to visit this place! Not only this, but it was also challenging for me to get into the small boats that would take us around the lake. Yet, it was a trip worth remembering and I was grateful for the opportunity to visit these countries, so far away from home.

In 2018, we undertook two amazing trips to the east. The first was to Japan and China and the other to Central Europe.

Tokyo is a very congested and expensive city to visit. The hotel we booked through the travel agency was clean and well-equipped but quite small compared to American standards. Whenever I had to go to the bathroom in the hotel room, I had to climb one step, forcing me to be extra cautious to avoid a fall. However, things were different in China. Our hotel was large and I had no difficulty there. We visited Shanghai, Chongqing, Xian, and Beijing. We also went on a cruise along the Yangtze River and visited the Three Gorges Dam. But there are lots of people in China! This was very apparent to me when we visited the Summer Palace, Tiananmen Square, and the Forbidden City in Beijing. The crowds were overwhelming and because of the rush, one has to move very fast. Thankfully, our tour guide had arranged for a wheelchair for me. The fellow who wheeled the chair was kind and helpful and stayed with me throughout the day.

In Central Europe, we visited the cities of Prague, Munich, Salzburg, Vienna, and Budapest. By this time, I was quite confident of walking on my own and faced no particular problems.

Most of my travels were organized by reputed travel agencies. The common aspect of these tours is that they have a fixed itinerary. There is some walking involved and one needs to keep up with the other tourists in the group. Some places have wheelchairs readily available, while others may not. For anyone in a similar situation, I only have one advice: it is sometimes okay to let go of an experience or excursion as I did near Peyote Lake in Canada and Bangkok, Thailand. This is for the best because not only is it for your safety, but also the convenience of others in the group. So, always listen to your tour guide and respect him or her. They are responsible for ensuring a seamless travel experience and need to maintain the timings of the tour. So if you cannot move fast enough or have difficulty in taking an early morning bus, it is better to refrain from taking these tours and instead go with a few friends or family at your own schedule.

11

EMBRACING A FIBER-RICH DIET

Dietary fiber is an important part of a well-balanced meal. Humans need between 25g to 35g of daily fiber intake to avoid any constipation. This is even more important when the body is fighting an ailment or medical condition as I am. The stroke brought many misfortunes in my life—an inability to walk properly, lack of good sleep, increased heart rate, and so on. It also affected the functioning of the smooth muscles—a type of muscles found in the walls of hollow organs like the stomach and intestine. The deterioration of this muscle type in the gastrointestinal tract may be the reason behind my intermittent heartburns and constipation.

To combat this, I closely monitor my fiber intake. For the last twelve years, every morning I drink a glass of water with a tablespoon of dextrin dissolved in it. Dextrin is nothing but an easy-to-digest soluble fiber. It is tasteless and has no side-effects.

In addition to this, I also include lots of fruits, vegetables, lentils, and whole grains in my diet. One of the best sources of fiber is found in prunes. I take about six every day. Another source of fiber is dried apricots—six of them yield about 3g of fiber (a little lesser than prunes of the same size).

I have learned from experience that there is no hard and fast rule for cooking. You are free to alter your cooking methods to suit your taste, as long as you keep your daily fiber intake constant. A high fiber diet not only increases your intestinal motility thus preventing constipation but also gives a sense of fullness. It also has the added benefit of removing unwanted elements such as high cholesterol from the body.

Here I share some of my favorite recipes. They are created to include adequate fiber intake.

Fiber in whole grains (in percentage)

Chia seeds	33% (5% soluble)
Bulgur wheat	18.3%
Rye	15.1%
Wheat	12.2%
Oats	10.6%
Freekeh	8.0%
Quinoa	7.0%
Couscous (semolina)	6.0%

Fiber content in various food items (grams/cup)

Prunes	12g
Apricots	8g
Raspberries	8g
Bran flakes	6.9g
Whole-wheat spaghetti (cooked)	6.3g
Barley (cooked)	6g
Pear (medium size)	5.5g

Fiber content in beans (grams/cup)

Split peas (boiled)	16.3g
Lentils (boiled)	15.6g (average)
Black beans (boiled)	15g
Lima beans (boiled)	13.2g
Green peas (frozen)	11.1g

Green peas (boiled)	8.8g

Tried and tested high-fiber recipes

In all the recipes given here, you can increase the water content by a few tablespoons, depending on the power of microwave used and personal preference in taste.

Cereal with Chia seeds
1 cup cereal of choice ¼ cup chia seeds 1 cup cold milk Mix all ingredients and enjoy a bowl of cereal enriched with extra fiber from the Chia seeds.

Whole wheat pancakes with raisins or peas

⅓ cup Krusteaz* honey-wheat or any whole wheat pancake mix
¼ cup water
⅓ cup sweetener (raisins or prunes or Craisins or frozen peas)**
1 tbsp olive oil

Substitutions:
* Substitute with any other whole pancake mix of your choice.

** Maple syrup is the more popular choice of sweetener. However, to reduce the caloric intake, I replace maple syrup with raisins, or Craisins (dried cranberries). If you want to use prunes, cut them into small pieces before adding them to the batter. Six prunes are adequate. If you want to completely cut down on sugar, you can use frozen peas instead. Simply thaw the peas in the microwave for 30 seconds.

In a bowl, mix the pancake mix with water.

Add your sweetener of choice. If you are using peas, you can add this at this time. Give the batter a quick stir so that everything is well-incorporated.

Heat oil on medium-high in a pan. Pour in the batter and let it spread out. When the pancake is set and the bottom has come loose, flip it, and reduce heat to about medium.

The pancake is ready when it no longer sticks to the pan.

Remove from pan and enjoy a wholesome breakfast.

Oatmeal with peas

⅓ cup precooked oats

⅓ cup frozen peas*

1 cup water

1 tsp olive oil

Salt and pepper to taste

* Thaw the peas in a microwave for 30 seconds.

Mix oats, water, oil, and peas in a microwave-proof bowl.

Put it into the microwave for two minutes.

Let it cool down for a few minutes and then enjoy your bowl of oatmeal with peas.

Oatmeal with milk

⅓ cup precooked oats
⅓ cup water
2/3 cup milk*

Mix the oats, water, and milk in a microwave-proof bowl.

Put it into the microwave for two minutes.

Let it cool down for a few minutes and then enjoy your bowl of oatmeal with milk.

Substitutions:

* Instead of milk, you can combine the oatmeal with six chopped-up prunes or apricots or one-third cup of Craisins or raisins or some nuts and a tablespoon of honey. If the consistency of the oatmeal is too thick, feel free to drizzle in a little milk before you eat.

Couscous or bulgur wheat with peas

⅓ cup couscous or fine bulgur wheat

⅓ cup frozen peas*

1 cup water

1 tbsp olive oil

Salt and pepper to taste

Mix all ingredients in a microwave-proof bowl.

Microwave it for three minutes.

Let it cool down for at least five minutes before eating. You can also transfer and spread it on a plate to allow it to cool faster.

Freekeh (or Kinoa) with peas

⅓ cup freekeh*
1 ½ cups water
⅓ cup frozen peas
1 tsp olive oil
Salt and pepper to taste

* Freekeh is a green grain made from young durum wheat. It is popular in many Arab countries and is readily available in Arabic ethnic food stores in the United States. Freekeh is very high in fiber content.

Wash the Freekeh thoroughly with water. Remove any floating grains.

Combine with water and microwave oven for 10 minutes.

Allow it cool for three minutes in the microwave. Then add the frozen peas, olive oil, salt, and pepper. Mix well. If it seems too thick, add a tablespoon of water to thin it down.

Heat it in the microwave for another 2 minutes.

Cool on the countertop for a couple of minutes. Freekeh with peas is now ready to eat.

You can easily substitute Freekeh with Kinoa (another fiber rich grain).

12

BE FINANCIALLY READY TO FACE EMERGENCIES

Medical emergencies come without a warning. No one can predict what the future hold and so it is prudent to be prepared financially for any eventualities. Otherwise, the burden of sorting out finances can fall on family members or loved once causing them additional harassment at an already trying time. In some cases, the patient may not even have someone close to relying upon to resolve any financial issues. I was fortunate to have the support of family and friends during and after my stroke. But I cannot stress enough the importance of being financially ready to face a life-threatening medical condition. From my experience, there are a few things of paramount importance that

I would like to discuss in this chapter. These factors will vary based on the disease and the country where the patient is located, but my experience is based in the United States so this chapter focuses mainly on American healthcare and insurance.

Medical insurance

Healthcare in the United States is one of the best in the world, but it is also the most expensive and that is why it is very important to have adequate medical insurance. For my total stay of forty-two days at various hospitals associated with the OSU, my medical insurance company was billed for about $400,000. There were also additional bills after my release from the hospital. The cost of the gamma knife surgery, performed four months after my release from the hospital, was about $50,000. The cost of therapy, a few Botox injections, and relearning driving was another $50,000. Out of a total of $500,000, I had to pay about $5,000 or one percent only (mainly for a copayment for therapy, Botox injections, and driving lessons). I had to pay so little because I was covered by medical insurance at work. I don't know how much my medical insurance company reimbursed the OSU hospital for my care. But, as far as I know, a medical insurance company never reimburses the hospital more than 25–50 percent of the billed amount, depending upon the volume of patients covered and contractual agreement.

Organizing documents

If you are incapacitated and not in a position to take decisions (as it was in my case), think about the trouble your family might have to face if they do not have access to relevant documents to take legal action on your behalf. A little organization on your part can do wonders for your family. It is also helpful to have a financial plan in place for health emergencies.

When I started working in 1976, I had one folder with the word "office" written on it. As my responsibilities grew in teaching, research, and administration, I began organizing my papers into separate folders. At the time of my stroke in 2008, I had forty to fifty folders, each containing documents about different aspects of my job—from individual graduate students to graduate studies committee, from individual research grants to research ideas, from promotion and tenure committee to medical education committees, and so on. Similarly, when we bought our first house in 1979, I had one folder called "home." This has grown to about sixty folders now. These folders individually contain miscellaneous information from cable TV subscriptions to financial investments to utilities. When I was unconscious after the stroke, these folders helped my wife immensely as she was able to decide on my behalf.

Ideas for folder organization

If you are new to experimenting with folder organization, here are a few handy folder ideas to get you started.

Credit card payments: If you do not have automatic withdrawal from your bank for credit card bill payment, you can write down the name of the credit card and payment due date because any missed payment can cost you a fortune.

Bank accounts: When I was in a coma for a few days, my wife needed some money. We have a saving account in a credit union but my wife could not remember which branch. She went from one branch to another to find the correct one and wasted a few hours in the process. It is, therefore, important to write down where your checking and savings accounts and other investments are and share this information with your partner. It is also helpful to file the paper statements in a relevant folder. Do online financial transactions only when both partners are comfortable with it. Otherwise, it is very difficult to know what the other may have spent online.

Financial documents: Source of income of both partners should be documented. If the income is directly deposited in the bank, it should also be mentioned. All monthly expenditures should be included including payment for the house, the insurance premium for house and car, utilities, taxes. If they are paid online, include relevant passwords. You should also keep a note of the names and contact details of financial professionals, such as financial advisers and estate attorneys, in a separate document.

Personal information: Keep a record of the personal information of each partner separately. Records of date of birth, social security, and mobile phone numbers as well as driving license card numbers and Medicare cards can be maintained.

Required Minimum Distribution (RMDs): If you have any tax-deferred investments, you have to withdraw RMDs after a certain age. Leave the proper information and take RMDs to avoid penalties from the Internal Revenue Service.

Revocable living trust: This allows you to take care of your financial matters as long as you are living and by a person appointed by you after your death. If you get incapacitated and are unable to make decisions, the person originally appointed by you can decide on your behalf. When you die, your family members can disperse your assets to listed beneficiaries.

What is the difference between a Will and a revocable Living Trust?

The main difference between a Will and a trust is that a Will goes into effect only after you die, while a trust takes effect as soon as you create it. A Will is a document that directs who will receive your property at your death whereas a trust can be used to begin distributing property before death, at death, or afterward. For example, you may set certain conditions in your Will that a listed beneficiary will receive your inheritance, only after he/she meets a criterion or achieves certain things. But who will decide if that person has achieved your listed criterion and should now get your inheritance? A revocable living trust allows you to give details of specific provisions when a particular beneficiary named by you receives an inheritance. For example, you may want a certain individual to receive half of your inheritance when they turn eighteen, and the other half after he/she finishes college education. The person appointed by you to take care of revocable living trust will make sure that your listed beneficiary has finished college education before he gets the other half of the inheritance. Without his/her approval, the listed beneficiary may not get the other half of the inheritance as requested. The trustee appointed by you can also make financial decisions for your underage children.

Legal matters

Will: You have to get an attorney's help to make a Will, a trust to disperse your assessments, and a durable power of attorney for your financial and legal matters in case you are not in a position to take any decision. The Will describes precisely who will get how much of your inheritance. You can make your own Will for less than $100 on websites such as <u>www. legalzoom.com</u>

A Living Will: This is a written document that will specify that in case of a health problem, what kind of medical treatment you want or don't want. It also includes the information on whether you want any heroic efforts on the part of health care workers beyond normal medical treatment. Let me explain this with a simple example. Supposing a patient is declared brain dead and kept alive solely with the help of artificial respiration. In such a scenario, should the patient be taken off support since there is no chance of brain activity revival? This can be enunciated in a Living Will that no such treatment is warranted. However, it is important to know that a Living Will does not affect the responsibility of medical care personnel to treat you fairly and properly.

Durable healthcare power of attorney: In case you are terminally ill or incapable of making your own decisions, the person who has been appointed by you previously as a durable power of attorney can decide what suitable medical treatment should be available to you. In my case, when I was in a coma incapable of making any decision, my son had the durable health power of attorney, and he decided whether my feeding tube should be inserted in my body through the trachea or abdomen. Because he is a medical professional, I was comfortable with appointing him as my durable healthcare power of attorney.

A durable power of attorney differs from a Living Will only in that the latter is a written document that specifies your wishes for medical treatment while the former allows the person appointed by you to decide for medical treatment for you on behalf. This person can also take financial decisions on your behalf if you are suffering from dementia or other medical issues that render you incapable of making rational financial decisions. Typically, no financial institution will reveal your financial information to anyone unless he/she can produce evidence that they have been legally appointed as your durable financial power of attorney.

In Ohio, if you are permanently incapacitated for making a decision, a Living Will declaration takes precedence over a durable healthcare power of attorney. However, both documents are the proper way to communicate with your medical staff about your medical procedure to them. However, it is important to know that as long as you are alive and capable of taking your own decision; your decisions supersede what is written in these documents. Some experts recommend that either you have a Living Will or durable healthcare power of attorney.

13

HEALING THROUGH PRAYER
AND GRATITUDE

I am not unknown to hardships and faced many struggles early in my life. I did not give up even when I realized that it was not going to be easy to tackle the aftermath of my stroke. Even so, it has not been an easy journey—not only physically but also emotionally.

Stroke is devastating because it is so sudden, and in most cases, comes with no warning signs. If you are lucky, you may wake up in the hospital but it also can mean coma or complete paralysis. When I woke up at the rehabilitation hospital, I had no recollection of what had happened or why I was at the hospital. It was very distressing, to say the least. I was also unprepared to deal with the mental trauma of the paralysis of the right side of my body. How does one go from being a healthy individual to one who is crippled, temporarily, or permanently? I asked myself "why me" over and over again. Unfortunately, there is no answer to this question. But to be well and recover mentally from the stroke, I knew I had to cope with the gravity of this question. For anyone else in this position, I will say only one thing: don't blame yourself for the misfortune of having a stroke and accept it as a part of your life—it has happened to you just as it might happen to anyone else. The acceptance that I was not to blame for my stroke gave me immense strength. And even though I had no underlying diseases or habits that could be seen as risk factors for a stroke, this acceptance did not come to me overnight. It took years of therapy and hard work on my part before I was truly able to realize it.

When I opened my eyes and regained senses at Dodd Hall, the first thought that came to my mind was that I was not sick and did not belong there. It took me a few days to understand the sequence of events as they took place on that fateful day. I recall thinking to myself that my life was over! I was semi-paralyzed. I could barely stand and thought I was wheelchair-bound forever. Not just that, even my speech was hard for others to understand. I presumed my teaching career was over and imagined that I would probably live in seclusion for the rest of my life with my wife in a remote place in India.

Having said that, I tried hard to keep a glimmer of hope alive in my heart. I wanted to believe that I would recover soon. Little did I know that my stay at the hospital would extend to forty-two days! I was supposed to teach a pharmacology course in the spring of 2009 and had no idea if I would recover by that time. Many gave false hope though not with malice. It was their way to uplift me. It was only my son, a doctor, who told me that I may or not recover completely. Naturally, I was disheartened to know this but in hindsight, he was correct.

An incident from my early post-stroke days merits a mention here. I had gone to vote on Election Day in Hillard. The booth was about a mile away from my home so I was able to walk with the help of a cane. There, I saw a middle-aged lady walking with a limp. She too had come to vote. On seeing her limp, I asked her what had happened. She replied that she had had a stroke about twelve years back. Her reply devastated me. And here I was hoping to get back to normalcy in six months! That was the first time I realized that I was in for a long haul. It was a frightening realization.

But, with time, I began to understand that recovery is not a destination; rather, it is a journey. It was only when I understood this that I found peace. While at the hospital, I used to constantly ask myself—why me? Why God was unkind to me? The first February after my stroke, I remember being at the hospital for my therapy session when suddenly a fire alarm went off. I was immediately wheeled out of the building by a staff member. It was -13 degrees Fahrenheit that day, and I simply could not bear the cold and broke down. In my head, unpleasant thoughts kept whirling—why did I suffer a stroke? How could I put myself in this situation?

It took me a few weeks of introspection when I realized that I did not *ask* for a stroke. It would have happened whether or not I wished for it. So, there was no point in berating myself for something I did not do. I had done nothing wrong. It could happen to anyone—you or me.

I also learned a few helpful things from the hospital staff. They would tell me to always remember that no two strokes are the same. Therefore, it was fruitless to compare two stroke victims. Just because one recovered quickly does not mean that another will too. The other thing they told me was that it was normal to be over-emotional after a stroke. Every individual has a different way of coping with stroke-related stress. Typically, it is seen that stress after a stroke can either induce anger or a tendency to cry easily. In my case, it was the latter. Even to this day, I become emotional, especially when narrating an incident about my stroke.

I must acknowledge that it was support from my friends and family that gave me the strength to recover from the stroke. During my initial days at the hospital, every morning I would eagerly wait for my wife to visit me. Only when she came would I brush my teeth and eat my breakfast. It was also the frequent visits from my son that were soothing to me. He lived in California and visited for six consecutive weekends until I was discharged from the hospital. Once I was discharged from the hospital, it was my wife who arranged for a wheelchair ramp to be built outside my house and get a temporary bathroom installed on the ground floor for me. But because she cannot drive, it was my friends who would drive her to the hospital daily, and also take me to the therapy hospital twice a week for six months straight till the time I was able to take the COTA bus for disabled people. I still feel emotional as I write these things.

At the rehabilitation hospital, I used to observe how others would cope with the stresses and strains of a stroke. One day, a young stroke patient, probably in his thirties, was brought to the therapy room for physical therapy. He was distraught and was shouting, "Leave me alone! God… I want to die… I wanted to die!" The incident reminded me of something I had read as a child. It said something like this: "If you want to be happy in life, just look at the people who are less fortunate than you are, in health, and have much less materialistic things than you have." Looking at that young patient, I realized that there were others worse off than me. Maybe even in physical pain. As for me, I had no pain, I was in familiar surroundings, and was well aware of the reason why I was at the hospital. Not only that, I had family and friends around me who were trying as hard as they could to help and support me. So, despite my misfortunes, there was a silver lining, and I knew I had to hold onto it.

After I was discharged from the rehabilitation hospital, I used to take a Central Ohio Transit Authority (COTA) bus to go for my therapy sessions to Martha More House or visit other hospitals. COTA runs special mini-buses for a nominal fee for disabled people. The COTA buses are run despite a big revenue loss to the company. For a minimal charge of only $3.50, it will take you anywhere in Franklin County. I once read in a local newspaper that the actual cost of running the COTA bus service is tenfold than what it charges its passengers! Even so, it is an extremely useful service not only for disabled people but also for their friends and family, who are freed up from the burden of driving them in town. Besides the low fare, one also has the privilege of meeting fellow (disabled) passengers. I probably never saw more than six passengers at a time on the bus, but I learned a lot about their health conditions and the difficulties faced by them.

The reason I mention the COTA service here is simply to demonstrate that no matter how hard my circumstances were after the stroke, I was still more fortunate than some others. When I started taking the COTA bus I was off the wheelchair and used to walk with the help of a cane. I needed no particular help to get on and off the bus. I met many disabled people who took the bus along with me. Many had multiple problems. Most of them were wheelchair-bound. Special equipment was used by the bus driver to secure their wheelchairs to the bus floor. One day, a fellow passenger looked like he had no particular problem. Curious, I struck a conversation with him and asked him as to why he was taking the COTA bus for the disabled. He told me that he had a failing kidney and was undergoing dialysis twice a week. His health condition looked frightening to me.

Since I traveled on the COTA bus on a set time and fixed days of the week, I generally met the same passengers all the time. I saw people with brain cancer who had undergone surgery and still had surgical scars on their skulls. I saw people who could barely stand and were wheelchair-bound forever. I even met people who barely spoke a word in English. Most passengers were silent, serious, and looked concerned, except for two young blind girls in their twenties.

The first time I saw them, they were busy chatting with each other and giggling. They were conversing about how mean their supervisor was and how they had to defend themselves from their supervisor's unnecessary demands. It occurred to me at that moment that I was sitting near two vibrant teenagers who were enthusiastic about their day to day life at their workplace. There was no shred of evidence that they were upset or uncomfortable at being blind. It made me realize that I could board the bus myself, I had no need for surgery or scars of any kind, and I could still see the world with my own eyes and appreciate it. If God has been that merciful to me by keeping me relatively unscathed, then what right I had to be sad and resentful, and ask God "why me?" I could complain that the right side of the body is weak or that I could not drive or write or run and blame God for my misfortunes, but what would I achieve through it? Instead, I learned to be grateful and thanked God that I could still eat and swallow, read and comprehend, work fulltime as a professor, take an hourly walk every day, and live a pain-free life. Ultimately, it was the belief in God that rescued me—God is my anchor. I no longer ask myself "why me?" Instead, I have learned to embrace my life and be grateful for the small and big blessings the Almighty has bestowed upon me.

Throughout my ordeal, if there was one person who stayed calm and level-headed, it was my wife. Instead of panicking, she focused on taking care of me. Every day for forty-two days, she visited me at the hospital without fail. It was only after I came home that I found the source of inner peace. It was a small prayer called *Mul Mantar* that she used to recite every day in the bed before we went to sleep.

Ik Onkar Satnaam Karta purakh Nirbhao Nirvairu Akal Murat Ajoonee Saibhan Gur prasaad

Jaap

Aad Sach Jugaad Sach,
Hai Bhi Sach Nanak hosee bhee Sach

Mul Mantar is the fundamental formula in Sikh religion and it summarizes the primary Sikh belief. The Punjabi word 'Mul' means, fundamental or root, and 'Mantar' means mantra or formula. *Siri Guru Granth Sahib* is the holy book of Sikhs, which was composed by Guru Nanak, the founder of Sikhism around the end of the fifteenth century. This holy book begins with a Sikh prayer called *Japji Sahib*. It is regarded as the most important *bani* or set of verses' in Sikhism, which is recited every day by the followers of this faith. *Japji Sahib* begins with the *Mul Mantar*.

The *Mul Mantar* has been widely debated for its exact meaning. Scholars of Sikhism differ in their interpretation of each word and overall message of it. I consider myself as the least qualified individual to clarify and explain it. However, the following is my understanding of the *Mul Mantar*.

> There is one universal creator called God. His name is truth.
> The creator is doer, fearless, he is not revengeful, unborn, self-existent, immortal, timeless, self-illuminated, known by the grace of Guru.
> It was true in the beginning, it is true today, and it will be true throughout ages.
> Oh Nanak, it will always be true.

My wife used to make me recite *Mul Mantar* daily. Through its recitation, I had a kind of self-awakening. Death is inevitable, and my stroke had, perhaps, taken me closer to it, even if momentarily. Then why worry so much about the misfortunes created by the stroke?

It was something that happened in my life over which I had no control. All I can do is to help myself, and by doing so, the creator will help me. The creator is my anchor, he is merciful, he is true and I have to have faith in submitting myself to his shelter.

In the beginning, I did not realize that prayer could motivate me to work harder. But it did. Not only did it have a positive impact on my everyday life, but it also made me stronger mentally and gave me the strength to work hard on myself. I was in a wheelchair for forty-two days in the hospital and at home for about two months. Then I gave up the wheelchair even though I could barely stand up. I started small and then started walking at a gradual pace.

I have always been more of a spiritual person than a religious one. But I am not dismissive of rituals and understand that they have an important role to play. All religions have some or other rituals. While some are more pronounced, others are subtle. Whatever the case may be, whether reciting a prayer or doing some other activity, a ritual brings discipline in life. In my opinion, there are three aspects of prayer: the act of recital, the faith in the Almighty, and the hard work. For a prayer to be effective, one must pay attention to all these aspects.

But prayer has no meaning without hard work. Merely reciting a prayer without taking necessary action will not be fruitful. Have you ever thought about how prayers work? The answer lies in the efforts one puts in *before* and *after* the prayer is complete. As a stroke victim, I might pray for good health but if after praying hard, I go out and gorge on sweets and junk food, will my prayer be answered? Or, if you have a job but don't work hard or take no initiatives; or, as a student do not study for your examinations— but simply pray to God, will you be successful? The answer to these questions is a resounding No. One must fulfill individual responsibility. Prayer alone will not work. There needs to be focus, initiative, and hard work. Just as a student must study hard to score well in an examination, a stroke patient must do his part by exercising regularly, sleeping well, and eating a healthy diet.

Medicines aside, all these things helped me on my road to recovery. There is no substitute for hard work, but prayer helped me focus and gratitude made me realize that no matter how much the hardship, there was always a silver lining and something to be thankful for each day.

CONCLUSION

I want to end this book by saying that a stroke does not have to be the end of the road. For anyone in a similar situation, know that there is hope. With therapy and consistent efforts, it is possible to fight the handicaps resulting from a stroke. But for this, it is important to be determined. No one can help you as much as yourself.

If you look around, millions of people have multiple medical problems. Remember that you are still better off than many. In my journey, I have learned to be grateful for what I have instead of blaming God or my destiny. When I used to take a COTA bus service for disabled people, I had the opportunity to meet other disabled persons. Some were disabled due to cancer; others were fighting kidney failure, and then those without sight. I realized then that many are battling far graver illnesses than I was. So why shouldn't I be grateful? Ultimately, you can either look at your circumstances as glass half-full or glass half-empty. The choice is yours. But I can say this with certainty that once you learn to see the glass half-full, your journey will become much easier.

I often ask myself, why we are here on the earth and in this universe. Our solar system depends on the sun at a distance of ninety-three million miles from the earth. But the sun is one of 10^{29} suns in this universe! That means it is one in a hundred billion trillion suns! It is very difficult for me to comprehend the vastness of our universe or fully understand our purpose on earth. All these things are beyond our control. I have learned to not worry about things beyond my control—just as I had no control over my stroke, even though it caused many problems for me. Instead of the "why me?" I have learned to ask "How can I overcome?" This is the question I am concerned about, and you should too. For example, if you have muscle weakness, try therapy. If you are suffering from constipation, increase your fiber intake. In short, be proactive in addressing your medical deficiencies.

The universe is about fourteen billion years old. If a human being is on earth for a hundred years, then it is a very short time when you look at the larger picture. Why worry about things you cannot control? Rather, focus on what you can control; for example, taking care of underlying causes of stroke or those resulting from it.

I have never been materialistic in my life. As long as I have food to sustain myself and shelter over my head, I am happy. This attitude has helped me immensely throughout my life.

I believe what our Holy Book, the *Bhagavad Gita*, states:

> What have you lost in life that you brought in this world? When you came into this world, you bring nothing. When you ultimately leave, you will take nothing. Whatever you have today belonged to someone else yesterday, and will

belong to someone else tomorrow. This is the rule of nature.

This means that we all come from the soil and return to it one day. So enjoy every moment in life, but do your duty. If nature is kind to you and you don't have to worry about floods or earthquakes or other disasters, then you must thank God for being merciful.

Remember to work hard and take care of your medical deficiencies that have occurred due to a stroke. With proper therapy and medical intervention, a stroke victim can recover and lead an almost normal life. Life may not run at a rapid pace but there is time to enjoy the fruits of life and live a joyful life.

The road ahead for me

Before the stroke, I taught pharmacology to medical students at the College of Medicine, the OSU, as well as undergraduate and graduate students across the campus. I would teach the course online for three quarters of the year and in the classroom one quarter of a year. After a six-month hiatus after my stroke,

I finally returned to teaching in June 2009. On the recommendation of my chairman, I started teaching pharmacology online, for all four quarters. This was the time when I could not drive and had to rely on the COTA Mainstream buses to reach the university. By teaching all four quarters online, I was granted a more flexible schedule as I no longer needed to reach work at a certain time of the day.

I continued teaching this way for four years after the stroke. However, I was finding it difficult to do certain things because of the weakness in my right part of the body. Finally, I decided to retire, and on July 1, 2012, I stepped down from active teaching and research.

Teaching was an integral part of my life and I enjoyed interacting with young students. So, I was happy when the OSU offered me a Faculty Emeritus title, an office space, and allowed me to teach a course, "Know Your Recreational Drugs" to undergraduate students. I now have a yearly contract with the OSU that can be extended indefinitely on a mutual consent basis. With the inclusion of this course, I have been teaching at the OSU for forty-four years as a regular or emeritus professor. Nowadays, I teach once a week on Wednesdays during the autumn semester.

With the outbreak of Coronavirus in the United States in 2020, the OSU was apprehensive but decided to keep the campus open for the fall semester of 2020. On-site teaching has resumed in the OSU but set guidelines on modes of teaching and social distancing protocol. I continue to take my once-a-week classes at the university. I have to wear a mask and so do all eighteen of my students. For eighteen students, the university has provided a large classroom that can accommodate a hundred students so that every student can maintain a social distance of six or more. If I touch a computer or anything else in the classroom, I have to use a hand sanitizer immediately. So far so good, and things are going well.

So, how has my life changed after the stroke?

To answer this question, I will go back to what I wrote about earlier—is the glass half-full or half-empty?

Because the life of a stroke patient comes to a screeching halt after a stroke, I'd like to think my glass is half empty. But the reality is not always as black and white.

I used to be a go-getter, vibrant, and never afraid of working hard. However, because of the physical limitation induced by the stroke, there are certain tasks I simply cannot do anymore. The most important thing for me is maintaining my balance. If I am not careful while walking on uneven surfaces or don't look down while walking, there are chances I may fall.

Fortunately, with time the balancing act has improved, and the rate of falling flat on the ground has improved from once every month to once every year. I take precautions and try to be watchful most of the time but an occasional fall is inevitable. For example, before getting out of bed in the morning, I sit on the edge of the bed for two minutes before standing up. This is to avoid any changes in my blood pressure due to orthostatic hypotension.

My weak right side means I have limited dexterity in my right hand. I cannot use the right hand to drive a vehicle and have to use a steering knob on the left side instead. Subtle movements of the hand and fingers required for using tools such as screwdrivers are also challenging for me. Even seemingly simple things like applying soap over my body are difficult. Because of the weakness in the right leg and the foot, running has become a vanishing dream.

But I still look at my glass as half-full. I have come back a long way since my stroke. When I was in the hospital and could not balance myself, three therapists or their assistants had to help me walk twenty steps. Now I can balance myself 99.9 percent of the time and walk one hour daily with the help of a cane. With time, I have improved in two avenues of life that please me the most. First is being able to write again. In the beginning, it was difficult for my thumb to meet the rest of my fingers in the right hand now I can sign checks, write short notes, and so on. Another satisfying improvement is my ability to drive again. Now I no longer need to depend on the COTA buses or seek help from my friends.

I am happy where I am in life now. I can do most of the things I could before the stroke, even if slowly and with some extra effort. I am surprised at how many day-to-day tasks I can do using my left hand. Twelve years back, I did not think it would be possible! When I wake up in the morning, I make my tea and breakfast. I read the newspaper and thank God that I can comprehend it. I can take a shower and change my clothes independently. I can even go out in foul weather and walk for one hour daily. I can drive comfortably and take my wife shopping. I can visit my friends for house parties or play cards with them. I can teach again and enjoy going to university. I can travel nationally and internationally.

OF course, now with the Coronavirus pandemic, we are mostly confined at home and strictly follow social guidelines for social distancing and wearing masks in public. Hopefully, one day we will be able to go back to our old schedule of enjoying a social life.

When I look at these things, I think, how lucky I am. God is great and helping me tremendously. What more can I ask for? I don't have to run all the time or move at a fast pace all the time. I just have to remember not to put myself in a situation that requires running! I never dreamed that a day will come again when I will be able to do everything again. Though there are some limitations, I have learned to accept them. For all the things that bring pleasure and independence in my life, I have to thank the Almighty for his infinite blessings.

ACKNOWLEDGMENTS

I want to thank my wife, Sarla, for her unconditional support. Without her, I would not have survived.

I want to thank my son, Samir, for his support, and the many trips he took from Ohio to California, to take care of me.

I also want to thank my friends for their unconditional support in helping me cope with my life-changing ordeal.

Last, but not least, I want to thank Arpita Dasgupta for professionally editing the manuscript.

Printed in the United States
By Bookmasters